PHYLLIS J. LE PEAU, BONNIE J. MILLER & NCF STAFF

HANDBOOK *FOR* CARING PEOPLE

With Questions for Individuals and Groups

CARING PEOPLE BIBLE STUDIES

INTERVARSITY PRESS
DOWNERS GROVE, ILLINOIS, USA
LEICESTER, ENGLAND

InterVarsity Press, USA, is the book-publishing division of InterVarsity Christian Fellowship, a student movement active on campus at hundreds of universities, colleges and schools of nursing in the United States of America, and a member movement of the International Fellowship of Evangelical Students. For information about local and regional activities, write Public Relations Dept., InterVarsity Christian Fellowship, 6400 Schroeder Rd., P.O. Box 7895, Madison, WI 53707-7895.

Inter-Varsity Press, UK, is the book-publishing division of the Universities and Colleges Christian Fellowship (formerly the Inter-Varsity Fellowship), a student movement linking Christian Unions in universities and colleges throughout the United Kingdom and the Republic of Ireland, and a member movement of the International Fellowship of Evangelical Students. For information about local and national activities write to UCCF, 38 De Montfort Street, Leicester LE1 7GP.

All Scripture quotations, unless otherwise indicated, are from the Holy Bible, New International Version. Copyright ©1973, 1978, International Bible Society. Used by permission of Zondervan Bible Publishers. Published in Great Britain by Hodder and Stoughton Ltd.

Much of the information in this book is taken from the Love That Heals Seminars and material produced by Bonnie J. Miller with permission from Nurses Christian Fellowship.

Chapter 3 is revised from "The Healing Effects of Forgiveness," by Phyllis J. Le Peau originally published in the Journal of Christian Nursing, Spring 1987.

Many of the ideas in chapter 5 are based on Spiritual Care by Judith Allen Shelly and Sharon Fish, 3rd ed., © 1988 and used by permission of InterVarsity Press.

Cover photograph: Michael Goss

USA ISBN 0-8308-1198-2
UK ISBN 0-85111-337-0

Printed in the United States of America

15	14	13	12	11	10	9	8	7	6	5	4	3	2	1
03	02	01	00	99	98	97	96	95	94	93	92	91		

1. Love That Heals ———————————————— 5

2. The Person God Uses ————————————— 11

3. Caring Through Forgiveness ———————————— 17

4. Communicating to People in Need ————————— 25

5. Caring for Spiritual Needs ———————————— 35

6. Caring for People Who Suffer ————————————— 45

7. Caring for People in Crisis ————————————— 53

8. Caring for People in Grief ———————————— 61

9. Letting God Care for Us ———————————— 69

10. Starting a Support Group ———————————— 79

Resource One: Record Keeping ———————————— 85

Resource Two: When Professional Help Is Needed —————— 87

Further Reading ———————————————— 89

1/Love That Heals

I sat motionless listening to every word. *The speakers affirmed what I knew in my own heart to be true.* The man who had now entered eternity was truly influential and a man of great wisdom and compassion. Joe Bayly had lived his life for God.

The Lord that Joe adored was the focus of this memorial service—full of worship and praise. His wife was surrounded by their children and grandchildren—a witness to God's faithfulness in their family. His books and articles had touched many people in the evangelical community. He was a well-known lecturer, a sought-after speaker and head of a major Christian publishing house. His ability to help Christians think through difficult issues was impressive.

But people didn't talk about his achievements or his titles or his fame. As I sat there taking it all in, one bold truth stood out—*Joe Bayly loved people!* When people spoke of how they had been touched by him, they simply told of the acts and words of kindness and generosity that had flowed from his life to theirs. As a result of his love, they had felt God's love. They had been healed, redeemed and given hope.

I left that service feeling a great surge of renewed meaning for my own life. Somehow I felt motivated, as never before, not to write books like Joe or even to become a lecturer, but to love as he loved—as Jesus loved. For when people had been with Joe, they felt like they had been with Jesus.

He Called Her "Daughter"

Two thousand years ago someone else found out what it is like to be with Jesus.

A crowd was following and pressing in on Jesus. In that crowd stood a woman whose period had not stopped for twelve years. She had suffered immensely. Though she had been under the care of many doctors, she got worse instead of better.

Somehow she knew that if she could just touch Jesus' clothes, she would be healed. Finally, she got close enough to him to touch his cloak. Immediately her bleeding stopped. She knew her suffering was over!

Jesus felt the power go out of him. Instead of ignoring her and going on his way, he asked, "Who touched me?" His disciples were astonished by his question. He was surrounded by a huge crowd. *Lots* of people had touched him!

But Jesus knew it was more than just being touched by a pressing crowd. He took the time to find out. The woman fell at his feet in weakness and fear. "Daughter," he said, "your faith has healed you. Go in peace and be freed from your suffering." "Daughter." Could he have spoken to her any more gently? Daughter. What an endearing term! He could not have more effectively communicated the value of her faith and his love for her. She left Jesus' presence healed, freed and in peace.

I, too, have known what it is to be in Jesus' presence. Being with him makes me want to obey him. Recently, I was feeling distressed, questioning if my energy was really being invested in the kind of work that would help to build Christ's kingdom. I wondered if I knew anything at all about being absorbed in God's focus for the world. I wrote in my prayer journal, "Lord Jesus, I *want* to know your will. I do not want to put my energy into anything less then your perfect will for me."

And then it struck me. I do not have to struggle with knowing God's will for me. He has clearly told me his will in Scripture. I am to love others (Jn 13:34-35; 15:12).

Love Releases Love

Imagine that you knew that you would die in a short time. Imagine also that those dearest and closest to you were around you ready to take in all that you were about to say. They know that their time with you is short. What would you want to talk about? My guess is that it would not be about the weather. Probably you would share the most important things in your life.

Jesus' last conversation with his disciples before his death is recorded in John 13—17. He is aware that the disciples will be holding on to every word and that what he says will be remembered long after his departure. Jesus speaks of what is most important to him.

Loving one another is the theme that occurs time and again throughout this discourse. He commands his followers to do it (13:34). He tells them how to do it—"as I have loved you." He even states that love is their identity, their "mark" as Christians. "By this all men will know that you are my disciples, if you love one another" (13:35).

Jesus didn't just give the instructions and go away. He, the Creator and loving Father, knew what his disciples needed to carry out his command. He made available to them his Holy Spirit as counselor, comforter and teacher. The Holy Spirit empowered them and empowers us. He confirms our love relationship with the Father and with the Son, and he enables us to develop the sensitivity to know the needs of others and to dare to meet them.

He also knew that to love others the disciples had to be loved themselves. In John 13 Jesus shows the "full extent of his love." He knew that the time of his death was near. Instead of being absorbed with himself, as we would be if we were going to die, he reaches out of himself to the disciples. He washes their feet, even the feet of the one who betrayed him.

When Peter did not have the foggiest idea what was going on, Jesus took the time to explain it to him. He met Peter at his level. He showed the disciples how to serve and love each other. And then he told them to do it. From washing feet to his cruel crucifixion, Jesus exemplified the extent of his love.

Joe Bayly knew deeply within his heart that God loved him. In the security of his love relationship with God he was freed to love others deeply. The woman who was bleeding knew that she was loved by Jesus. The disciples who would be used to turn the world upside down with the good news of

Jesus' love, first knew that God loved them. Love releases love.

Learning to Love

Love is what this book and the Caring People Bible Studies are all about. Loving God. Being loved by God. And loving each other. Loving those in need. We all need to be loved. And this handbook will get you started.

The next two chapters look at who we need to be as caring people. After that we will look at communicating to people in need, caring in crisis, visitation programs and how to let God care for you. Much of what is found here originated in a seminar from Nurses Christian Fellowship called "Love That Heals" that was developed by Bonnie Miller. This book, like the seminar, is for ordinary people like you who want to know more about caring for people in practical and genuine ways.

There are also seven Bible study guides in the Caring People series. These studies look at what the Scriptures say concerning caring for others. The guides cover caring for people in grief, conflict, spiritual need, emotional need and physical need as well as the character and resources of caring people. Suggestions for further study at the end of each of the chapters in this book list the guides with studies which are relevant to the topic in the chapter.

This book can be of use to individuals or groups. Discussion questions for an individual or a group are found at the end of chapters 1—9. There are also suggestions for forming and organizing groups who desire to focus on caring for people in need in chapter 10. The care and support of our Christian community is essential as we undertake this vital ministry of becoming caring people.

May the God of peace and hope bless you as you grow in becoming caring people.

Questions for Individuals or Groups

1. How would you define love?

2. Think of someone you know who does not seem to know experientially that God loves him or her. How do you see this in that person's life?

3. Think of someone you know who seems to personally and continually experience God's love. How do you see this in that person's life?

4. How have you personally been affected by someone who is secure in God's love?

5. How do you respond to the fact that Jesus demonstrated his love through teaching, washing the disciples' feet, and reaching out to others at a time when he could have been totally absorbed in his own death?

6. What do you think you need to experience a more intimate and secure relationship with God?

7. What role has Christian community played in your experience of being aware of God's love?

8. How do you see the relationship between being loved by God, loving God and loving others?

2/The Person God Uses

The fact that you are reading this book shows that you want to be used by God and learn more about caring for others. God calls you to love others and equips you for that task. He wants to make you into a person he can use.

How God Communicates to Us

Jesus is our model of caring. He came, lived and ministered among us. He didn't stand at a distance and throw out pious phrases. He was actively involved in people's lives. By doing this he communicated who God is. We are supposed to do the same. If Jesus' love is in us, the people we care for are in a real way being cared for by Jesus.

The big difference, of course, is that Jesus is perfect but we are in process. We are becoming like Jesus. The process will not be complete until we get to heaven. Many of us feel like real beginners in this ministry of caring for others. And that's all right. We can identify with the disciples as they began their ministry and learned from Jesus as he taught them!

Jesus launched his ministry with the knowledge that he was loved by his father. The people God can most freely use are those who *know* that God loves them. God made his love very clear to Jesus with his words, "You are my Son, whom I love; with you I am well pleased" (Mk 1:11). God also tells us very clearly that he loves and accepts us. He does this through his people, his creation, his Spirit and his Word.

I am very grateful for God's people. I am thankful for those that have touched me deeply in my lifetime and have demonstrated God's love. But I am also grateful for those in history who faithfully lived and proclaimed the truth of God's love. The message reached me because they were faithful.

Creation explodes with God's love. This message is clearly stated in the words of a beloved hymn, "Summer and winter, and springtime and harvest. Sun, moon and stars in their courses above. Join with all nature in manifold witness, to thy great faithfulness, mercy and love."

God meets our physical needs of food and shelter with his creation. The beauty of creation soothes our emotions in an elegant way. God moves our spirits toward himself through creation: "what can be known by God is plain to them because God has made it plain to them. For since the creation of the world God's invisible qualities—his eternal power and divine nature—have been clearly seen, being understood from what has been made" (Rom 1:19-20).

The Spirit of God is our Comforter. He convicts us of sin and moves us in the right direction. The Holy Spirit is the one that convinces us of Jesus' righteousness. The Spirit of God will never leave us. He is God present with us and presence communicates love. He is the Spirit of truth and reminds us of the truth of what we believe. Jesus expressed his love for us by saying, "I will not leave you as orphans. I will ask the Father, and he will give you another Counselor to be with you forever—the Spirit of truth" (Jn 14:16-18).

The Word of God is full of expressions of love to us. Just a few of them are:

☐ I made you (Gen 1:26; Ps 139:13-14).

☐ I know all about you (Ps 139:14-16, 26).

☐ I care for you (Ps 103:13-14; Ps 145:15-16).

☐ I have called you by name and redeemed you (Is 43:1; 1 Pet 2:9-10).

☐ I will continue to redeem you (Eph 1:3-4; Phil 1:6).

☐ I love you (Is 43:5).

☐ You are precious and honored (Is 43).

☐ You are accepted and forgiven (Rom 8:1; 14:3; 15:7).

☐ You are my workmanship, in process (Phil 1:6).

We need to choose to believe our Father's expressions of his love. Our relationship with God is based on this truth from Scripture. We must saturate ourselves with the Word of his love to confirm that love in our hearts.

How We Love Others

Loving others flows out of our being loved by God. This motivation is in contrast to being motivated to do his work in order to gain his favor. We have been transformed by his love, and we want others to be transformed by it too. When we know that we are loved and valued by him, we are freed to share our lives with others. We are safe with him—what harm can others do to us?

Something else that flows out of this loving relationship with God is our ability to accept ourselves just as God accepts us—with our gifts, limitations, health, body, appearance, sexuality and temptations. The foundation we can build the acceptance of ourselves on is God's love, acceptance and forgiveness.

Jesus himself knew this kind of inward security because of his relationship with his Father. Jesus knew who he was, the power he had in the Father and where he was going (Jn 13:3). He made himself extremely vulnerable and available for service. He felt free to strip to the waist to wash the disciples' feet the night before he died.

Jesus was also open in the way he talked. He came to this earth as the Word—and cared for his disciples by communicating with them unguardedly. He told them who he was and of their value to him. He allowed them to see his feelings and his tears. He spoke of his purpose and plan for them.

Open and honest communication is a rare commodity these days. However, talking openly and being vulnerable is vital for people who are caring for others.

Jesus was perfect. We are broken and hurting people with a propensity to sin. But in Christ we are the children of God and are able to participate in the divine nature of Christ (2 Pet 1:4). As we grow in this process of accepting ourselves, we grow in loving and accepting others. The end result is that we "love our neighbors as ourselves" (Mk 12:31).

Resources for Loving

The people God uses to love others find their strength and priorities in God.

It seems that every time Jesus had important decisions to make he spent long periods alone with his Father. In Mark 1:35 it says he got up very early in the morning and went to a solitary place to pray. He must have done it quite regularly for the disciples knew exactly where to find him.

In our world it is difficult to be quiet and to listen to God. Life is full of activity—fix-it projects, church meetings, business trips, letters to write; even recreation like going to movies or plays or sporting events or weekends away can be wearing at the frantic pace we sometimes maintain. We are addicted to so much activity because we need to prove our own worth or want to run away from our lack of self-worth.

It is hard to choose to set aside the time of quiet that is needed to hear the still small voice of the Spirit of God. It is even more difficult to do it. When we don't, the temptation is to go in our own direction on our own strength instead of going in the more certain direction and more powerful strength of the Holy Spirit.

Strikingly, it was the hassled and excited disciples who interrupted Jesus' quiet time to let him know that he was in demand. Everyone was looking for him! (Mk 1:37). But Jesus was not distracted from the sense of purpose and priority that flowed from his time alone in prayer. He didn't bend to those demands, but told the disciples they needed to go to new villages to preach (Mk 1:38-39).

We desperately need to have God's priorities. The needs in this fallen and broken world could swallow us up if we move out without God's strength and direction. Jesus knew how to say no. He did not meet all the needs around him. He did not respond to every call to come. He certainly did not intervene automatically to reverse everyone's difficult situation. When we are tempted to volunteer for every committee, answer every plea for help we hear on the phone, and rescue every friend in need, we need to ask if this is God's ministry for us. If not, like Jesus, we should say no.

Another of Jesus' resources was his team. So the people God uses are those who do not minister alone but with the support of others. In Mark 1:16-20, very early in his public ministry, Jesus called his first four disciples. He did not try to "go it" alone. He developed a team to work and fellowship with. He trained his team, and they took over the task after he was gone.

As you become involved in caring for others, think of yourself as a person on Jesus' team now being trained to carry on his work. Learning from others, supporting one another and training others are just a few of the elements of a Christian community. We cannot do effective ministry as "lone rangers." One way of ministering in a team is to start a group of people who are committed to caring for others in need (see chapter ten).

Being a team member is not necessarily easy. From single-serving cans of soup to making career decisions without taking into account friends or family, our world reinforces individualistic living. In *Defeating the Dragons of the World*, Stephen Eyre writes that the creed of this dragon of individualism is, "I am the source of my own value." This dragon seats itself firmly in our minds and locks us inside ourselves and locks others out.

Seeing what Jesus is doing for me is a vital resource for being a caring person. Do I see Jesus taking me by the hand and "raising me up" from whatever is immobilizing me? As I see this in my own life I can carry this hope to others. I need the conviction that Jesus is in control over the effects of brokenness in my life and in the people I care for. Even the evil spirits cried out in recognition of "Jesus of Nazareth, the Holy One of God" and of his power over evil.

Throughout the New Testament, the words "filled with compassion" (Mk 1:41) are used to describe Jesus. We see this compassion demonstrated here when he healed a man with leprosy. He is not only willing, but *wants* to touch those scarred parts of our lives and free us to love others with his compassion. We cannot produce his compassion in ourselves. It is up to the Holy Spirit to make us into the compassionate person that God uses.

As we grow in becoming the person God uses by struggling with our own needs and weaknesses and failures, hear the words of the apostle Paul:

Not that I have already obtained all this, or have already been made perfect, but I press on to take hold of that for which Christ Jesus took hold of me. Brothers, I do not consider myself yet to have taken hold of it. But one thing I do: Forgetting what is behind and straining toward what is ahead, I press on toward the goal to win the prize for which God has called me heavenward in Christ Jesus. (Phil 3:12-14)

Questions for Groups or Individuals

1. Much of this chapter is based on Mark 1:1-45 (especially the resources for loving). What qualities of Jesus do you see in this passage that stand out to you? Why?

2. Which of these qualities do you feel are strongest in you? weakest? Explain.

3. How do you rate yourself on a scale from 1 to 10 (10 being loving yourself a lot) in the area of loving yourself? Explain.

4. Why do you think you do or do not accept yourself?

5. How do you see the effects of accepting yourself in relationships with others?

6. How do you respond to God's words of love to you that you read in this chapter?

7. In what ways are we becoming like Jesus?

8. How would you describe your patterns of Bible study and prayer? Specifically, how would you like them to change?

For Further Study:

The Character of Caring People, Resources for Caring People.

3/Caring Through Forgiveness

I trusted Karen. We had shared a lot of life—dormitory days in nursing school, very difficult clinical instructors, the death of her grandfather, Karen's becoming a Christian, exciting Bible studies, a Nurses Christian Fellowship leadership conference, praying together, fun times, and even the pain of a man I loved walking out of my life. She was one of the first people with whom I became vulnerable. She was my dearest friend.

We made plans to move to Southern Illinois University together to finish work on our degrees in nursing. Suddenly Karen changed her mind. It was more convenient for her to stay where she was. I felt unimportant and betrayed. My hurt turned to anger and the anger, unresolved, to bitterness. No matter what she did to try to make the relationship right, I was determined she would never hurt me again.

That led to the darkest hour of my life. Darkest, not because of what Karen did, but because I refused to forgive. The author of Hebrews talks about the root of bitterness that springs up and causes trouble and by it many become defiled (Heb 12:15). I experienced that destruction. I was depressed. I lost too much weight. I was ineffective in my nursing.

I was consumed with the hurt—and so were Karen and many others around us. Our roommates felt the tension. People we worked with at the hospital were hurt by the tension in our relationship. Bible studies lost their effectiveness. A relationship which had been a bright testimony of sisters walking together in unity and outreach to others now became a detriment to the gospel message.

I knew what Scripture taught about reconciliation. I knew what I should do. But I chose not to obey. I simply would not run the risk of being hurt again. In the whole process, supposedly protecting myself, I was hurting myself much more, along with many others.

I am not alone. Struggling with hurt and anger is the norm for many people. Bitterness and a refusal to forgive is at the root of much physical as well as spiritual and emotional illness, and so it is at the core of many of the needs of people you are called to care for.

We are devoting a whole chapter on this subject for two reasons. The first has already been illustrated—bitterness is the cause for much suffering. The second reason is you must be a forgiving person yourself in order to help others learn how to forgive. The very foundation of my ability to forgive is the fact that God has forgiven me.

God's Reconciliation

God reconciled all things to himself through Jesus' death on the cross (Col 1:19-22). The result of this reconciliation, according to Paul, is that we are presented before God holy and blameless and beyond reproach. It is very exciting to me that God not only did this but that he was *pleased* to do it. We were his enemies and he made us his friends! He took the initiative. He paid the price.

I was not able to forgive Karen until I realized how dreadful *my* sin was. When my eyes were opened to my serious offenses against Jesus Christ and to the extent of his forgiveness to me, I knew how minimal Karen's offenses were. I began to experience the grace of God in a deep way. As I meditated on the cross and Jesus' gruesome death there for my sin, my pride, my hatred, my jealousy, my uncontrolled tongue, my bad thoughts, my selfish attitudes, I was not only able to forgive Karen, but I experienced the gospel in a way I had not experienced it before.

The Scriptures also say that because God has made us his friends he has given to us the message of reconciliation. We can care for others by proclaiming to them: "I have been reconciled to God through Jesus Christ! You too can be forgiven. And we can be reconciled to each other. We can even be reconciled to our pasts and to our future."

What more effective way is there to proclaim this message than by demonstrating God's forgiveness by forgiving others? We are to live out this message in relationship to other people, not only out of gratitude for God's forgiveness but also because God commands us to forgive others. Matthew 6:14-15 states: "For if you forgive men when they sin against you, your heavenly Father will also forgive you. But if you do not forgive men their sins, your heavenly Father will not forgive your sins."

Because it took me years to come to this point of brokenness and obedience in my relationship with Karen, there was great damage in that relationship to be dealt with. Damage that could have been avoided if I had simply obeyed God.

When Obedience Is Tough

A life of forgiveness and of freedom from bitterness is the only way to live. But I am certainly not suggesting that living this way is magical or even easy. Obedience to God is rarely easy. It often rubs against the very grain of our natural inclination.

There are times when I do not feel like forgiving. There is one bit of premarital counseling that I remember most. That counsel was that Andy and I should never withhold forgiveness from one another. That certainly hit a tender nerve because of what had happened with Karen. We promised each other that we would always forgive. This is one important reason why our marriage has remained healthy and growing.

When I do not feel like forgiving, I try to consider why. Is it a power play? Do I gain certain satisfaction from holding something over his head? Am I making him pay for what he has done? Am I afraid of being hurt again? Do I feel a sense of pride or superiority, a feeling that I would never do anything like that?

Often, just being able to put my finger on the reason for a feeling helps to lessen its control over me. But regardless of the reason or whether or not I know what the reason is, my life does not need to be controlled by feelings.

Love is much more than an emotion. Forgiving is much more than feeling like doing it. I would suspect that in his agony on the cross, Jesus did not feel like forgiving. Obedience is an act of the will. When I obey the command to forgive (and relate to that person as if the offense had not occurred), I have found that often the feelings follow.

Meditating on the fact that I have been forgiven by God motivates my obedience. The degree to which someone has wronged me lies in stark contrast to the degree I have sinned against God. My offense is overwhelmingly greater. Yet he forgives again and again. And he relates to me as though the offense had never occurred.

I am still basking in such a recent experience with God. I had been unreasonably angry with the children. Their actions were not nearly as bad as the intensity of my anger indicated. Before the Lord I wept. The sense of failure overwhelmed me like the waves of the ocean when the tide shifts unexpectedly. Had it been my first time of coming to the Lord with such a situation, it might not have been so painful. But because it had happened so many times, I asked in desperation, "Can I really start over with you again? Can you forgive me? This has happened so often." And the answer yes from him was loud and clear and as refreshing as playing in those same ocean waves when all is well. My children forgave me again too.

Considering the consequences of not forgiving is also helpful in the battle with feelings. Refusing to forgive simply means continuing with a broken relationship, giving up peace with God, damaging our health. Nothing is accomplished by not forgiving.

A friend of mine cannot forgive her mother. There is no question that Mary's mother has failed in being the kind of Mom that Mary needed. She made little or no effort to spend time with Mary as she grew up other than doing the routine maintenance care. Mary was a great basketball player in high school. Her mother did not see her play once. She gave little or no affirmation to Mary as a person or for her accomplishments. She did not express love, at least not verbally. Her mother responded to important decisions in her life with apathy. Even in adulthood, Mary's mother continued to manipulate her and attempt to mold her into an "acceptable" person. She gave gifts to Mary but then used them as a tool to try to get what she wanted.

Mary's mother does not acknowledge that she has wronged her. She may not even be aware of it. She certainly has not asked for forgiveness. The hostility and bitterness in Mary's heart continues and the hardness that results is making her into the type of person her mother is. Though her mother is close to death, Mary continues to withdraw from her. If Mary would forgive her mother, she would experience freedom and joy. Instead Mary is experiencing indifference and anger and hardness of heart.

Forgiveness Is a Process

What happens when I forgive or am forgiven? There are several things that take place when I forgive someone. Most important of all, I am obeying God. I am pleasing God. I am humbling myself when I forgive. I am giving up a certain control over that person. Even if the person does not ask for forgiveness, I am making the difficult choice to forgive.

I still feel the effects of being forgiven by my sister years ago. I was very jealous that she always had dates. After all, she was two years younger and attracted the young men I would like to date. My anger and cruel treatment of her was met by unsolicited forgiveness and graciousness.

Granting forgiveness heals and builds trust. It even affects other relationships. My heart is softened, and I am more willing to be vulnerable with others when I have been truly forgiven.

In thinking through the process of forgiveness, I see two potential problems—not forgiving someone else and that person not forgiving me. Possibly the second is the most painful because I feel so totally out of control when this happens. I experience pain when I confess the wrong, and the person will not forgive.

If I have done all in my power to get things right, and that person does not forgive me, I can pray for him or her. Job prayed for the "friends" that had tormented him. I am not speaking of a casual prayer request—he labored before God. The restoration process is greatly helped when I pray fervently for the person who will not forgive me. It is difficult for bitterness to grow in my heart when I am genuinely praying for that person.

God answers prayer. Much of the credit in the restoration of my relationship with Karen when I was not willing to forgive goes to God responding to Karen's faithful praying.

My prayer is, "Please grant healing. Give them the strength to obey you." I also ask God to keep my heart from bitterness and to help me respond as Jesus would. Jesus was falsely accused before many but did not open his mouth in defending himself.

How do I pick up the pieces when forgiveness is granted? There is an old saying, "To forgive is to forget." That is not necessarily true. Sometimes Andy and I experience what we call "fall out." These are times when memories of the pain remain, though forgiveness has been granted. Because forgetting does not necessarily happen immediately, we do not measure our forgiveness by loss of memory. Forgiving involves making a choice about what I do with what I remember. I *choose not to* dwell on the incident as I did before or to use it against that person. I *choose to* relate to that person as if he or she had never sinned.

Preventative Measures

How do I keep relationships from getting so bad that it is very difficult to forgive? Talk, talk, talk. Listen, listen, listen. So much hurt, so much resentment is due to lack of communication. The Scripture is both wise and practical when it says to not let the sun go down on your wrath. Resolving problems when they are small problems is much easier than when they are allowed to grow big.

Sometimes I have to go to Andy even when I know the irritation is my problem. Talking helps me to resolve *my* internal conflict. I need to do this when I cannot just talk myself out of it.

There are also times when Andy may be the guilty party but the offense is very small. I am embarrassed because I am not able to overlook it. Talking honestly about my feelings, however, and listening attentively to him brings increased understanding and resolution.

Feelings that are not discussed but are repressed will push up their ugly heads at any given opportunity. This is especially true when circumstances similar to the original hurt occur. You need to be aware of this possibility in those you are caring for. Many hurting people are living with bitterness.

Again it is the practicality and wisdom of Scripture that sets the pace for us. In Matthew 18:15 it tells me to go to my brother if he sins against me, and in Matthew 5:23-24 to go to my brother if I sin against him. So in both cases going to settle with my brother or sister is *my* responsibility. I *cannot* wait for them to come to me. There is too much at stake.

Forgiving Yourself

A final practical point concerning forgiveness is that I must be able to forgive myself. Satan is the accuser of the brethren. He knows that one of his greatest tools against the believer is guilt. He accuses us constantly. He will even stoop to stirring up guilt over offenses already forgiven by God, to keep us oppressed and defeated. There are many people who are living under the bondage of false guilt. False guilt has another side effect; it can deter an individual from dealing with real guilt that results from sin.

We must live and help others to live with a true perception of God's grace and forgiveness. The liberating message of the gospel of Jesus Christ is, "I am forgiven." A liberating life of forgiveness is the only way to live. As Paul said, "Be kind and compassionate to one another, forgiving each other, as in Christ God forgave you" (Eph 4:32).

Last night the phone rang. It was Karen. She was weeping and told me of Mom Schurman's death. She called because she knew I cared and would understand.

I cried too. I wept because I grieved with her. But my tears were also tears of joy and gratitude. The call reminded me of the healing and restoration that had taken place in a once shattered and broken relationship. The freedom of forgiveness and reconciliation is possible through the power of the gospel of Jesus Christ. We can and must take Jesus and his good news of forgiveness, peace and healing to broken people in our broken world.

Questions for Groups or Individuals

1. What does it mean to you that God has forgiven you?

2. In what ways do you have difficulty believing God's forgiveness of you?

3. When have you struggled with forgiving another person? What did it feel like?

4. How do you think God's forgiving you affects the way you forgive others?

5. What has been your experience in praying for someone who has hurt you?

6. Think of a person that you care for who may be struggling with forgiving someone. What are the symptoms of this lack of reconciliation?

7. What are some of the misconceptions that people have about forgiveness?

8. What are the ways that you can communicate the message of God's forgiveness to others?

For Further Study:

Caring for People in Conflict.

4/Communicating to People in Need

argery Williams, in The Velveteen Rabbit, *tells the story of the splendid gift a young boy received at Christmas—a beautiful stuffed rabbit covered with velvet.* Unfortunately, after a couple of hours of attention on Christmas day the little rabbit was shoved off into the toy closet and pretty much ignored by everyone. The more expensive toys snubbed him and the mechanical toys acted very superior, looking down upon everyone else. They were full of modern ideas and pretended that they were real.

Since the velveteen rabbit did not know that real rabbits existed, he could not pretend to be anything. But the Skin Horse, who had lived in the boy's room longer than any of the other toys, was kind to him. He had watched many mechanical toys come and go and knew that they would be nothing else but toys.

"What is REAL?" asked the Rabbit one day, when they were lying side by side near the nursery fender. "Does it mean having things that buzz inside you and a stick out handle?"

"Real isn't how you are made," said the Skin Horse. "It's a thing that happens to you. When a child loves you for a long, long time, not just to play with, but REALLY loves you, then you become Real."

"Does it hurt?" asked the Rabbit.

"Sometimes," said the Skin Horse, for he was always truthful. "When you are Real you don't mind being hurt."

"Does it happen all at once, like being wound up," he asked, "or bit by bit?"

"It doesn't happen all at once," said the Skin Horse. "You *become*. It takes a long time. That's why it doesn't often happen to people who break easily, or have sharp edges, or who have to be carefully kept. Generally, by the time you are Real, most of your hair has been loved off, and your eyes drop out and you get loose in the joints and very shabby. But these things don't matter at all, because once you are Real you can't be ugly, except to people who don't understand."

Eventually the velveteen rabbit was loved, REALLY loved by the young boy. He lost his hair and became very shabby in the process. But the little rabbit was so happy that he didn't even notice what was happening to his beautiful velveteen hair or that the pink was being rubbed off of his nose where the little boy had kissed him. He became real to the little boy. And in the end he became real, not only to the boy—but to everyone.

For me, the process of becoming real began when a friend cared about me enough to get beyond my false front to the *real* me. Part of my pretense was that I had it all together. I felt this image was important to represent God adequately to others.

And yes, becoming real was painful. But, as the wise old Skin Horse said, "When you are Real you don't mind being hurt," and it was certainly worth it. At first I didn't like my shabbiness and loose joints becoming obvious. There are still times that I'd rather be "full of modern ideas" and have "stick out handles and things that buzz inside me."

But my friend continued to love me. She did not even notice the shabbiness. Because I was accepted, I was freed to become more real. First to her and then to others. For as she listened to me, really listened and accepted me, I also experienced God's love and acceptance in a new way. As she asked questions and then shared herself, I discovered I did not have to deny my own humanity and needs to be an acceptable Christian.

I found out that God's reputation was not at risk because of my brokenness. In fact as I was able to become more honest and vulnerable, God's redeeming work in me became more obvious, both to me and to others. The emphasis moved from *me* having it all together to *God* having it all together.

Much of the pain in life is trying to be something that I am not. This dissatisfaction is often at the core of people's needs. Knowing that I am valued by God just like I am is what "real" is all about.

Communicating Makes Us Real

One way that a person becomes real is through loving communication. In this way we give to others the freedom and the permission to be real. Dialogue is becoming a lost art in our modern, technological and fast-paced society. People crave to be cared about. They want to be listened to. They want someone to respond to them and to talk about what is really important to them. They long for intimacy with God and with others.

Ruel Howe says in his book *The Miracle of Dialogue*, "As blood is to the cell, dialogue is to love." Think about what happens to a cell when the blood supply is cut off. Oxygen and nutrients can not reach this cell. Toxins and waste products will not be carried away. The cell will quickly shrivel up and die. And so it is with love. For love to thrive and grow and be healthy in any relationship, communication is essential.

Communication is not just a way of using words—it is a lifestyle. Instead of withdrawing from one another and from God as Adam and Eve did after they sinned, we open ourselves up to each other and to God. We then experience his love and forgiveness. We communicate his love. We can help others to experience their redemption more fully—or to desire to be redeemed in the first place. This is our goal.

I grew up in a family that loves and accepts me. They communicated God's love to me. When I was a child, they listened to me. My opinions were valued. I used to take this for granted, but I don't anymore.

I continually meet people who did not have this gift as they grew up. They did not feel loved. As a result, they have great difficulty being able to trust God or trust people. They are afraid to communicate their needs. They protect themselves from further hurt by hiding from others.

We communicate acceptance to others by asking people questions about themselves and then listening very carefully. People do not generally talk about themselves unless they are asked. We are also wrong to assume that we know their motives and feelings. It is extremely difficult but extremely important to let people express themselves fully before we start talking. "I cannot hear what you are saying because of what I think you are going to say" is an enemy of effective dialogue. The process of self-awareness and self-acceptance continues through dialogue with others in a safe relationship.

I am amazed at the profound effect of God's love and acceptance on people. When I was a freshman in the school of nursing, the upperclassmen who were Christians prayed for us by name before we even got there. When we arrived, we were met with care and individual attention. This acceptance was completely new to some. As a result, they were freed to show more of themselves and to admit their needs. The environment was set for the great spiritual and emotional growth that took place as many became Christians.

When the needs are obvious, people are still reluctant to let you into their lives unless they sense you won't judge them or be shocked. Creating trust is even more critical when the needs are deeply hidden. People may test us first with stories of "friends" or with their minor problems. They watch our reaction very closely to see if they can safely share more.

How to Communicate
Sensitive questions, touch, time, active listening, and appropriately sharing ourselves are some of the ingredients of communication that help this "openness" to happen.

Although there can be certain circumstances in which monologue is appropriate (such as a speech, a lecture or a sermon), in conversation a monologue is deadly. Some may talk incessantly and not even be aware that they are monopolizing the conversation. This easily happens when people are full of fear and anxiety.

Dialogue, on the other hand, is a flow of meaning. Just as blood flows to and from the cells, dialogue flows between people. In this flow I am seeking to give myself to others even as I am seeking to know others as they are. True dialogue goes beyond speech. It is not a method but rather a principle of living.

Dialogue means being genuine, authentic and open. We are in touch with our own feelings, able to give and to receive from others undefensively. Because we do not need to defend themselves, we do not even have to be understood by others.

Dialogue takes discipline. We can't be content to just let life and relationships happen. We think through relationships, plan a healthy approach, pray about other's needs as well as our own and evaluate how this caring relationship is going.

God is our role model for communication. He freely expresses to us his love with words, and through the Word, Jesus Christ. He also communicates through his actions. He created the universe, and he created us. He allows us to oversee his creation. He gives us good work to do. His ultimate act was sending his Son, Jesus Christ—not only as the Redeemer but also as the Word—the revelation of God himself to our world.

Steps to Good Communication

Communication does not just happen. There are basic steps. The first is *to openly and honestly express myself to others*. To do this we need nonjudgmental listeners, and we need courage. We all to some degree or another fear that what we say could be used against us.

My small group helps me in this process of becoming real that began so long ago. We laugh and sing and celebrate together. We even eat together. But we also weep and admit wrong and failure and weakness and struggle and we love and pray for each other. I do not have to worry about losing their love or respect because I struggle. They continue to love me in spite of the shabbiness and failure. They remind me of God's love and forgiveness.

The second step to communication is *to listen to others*. Listening may seem passive, but it is not. Active listening means listening for meaning and feelings as well as to the facts that are being spoken without judgment. Listening begins with questions, but then the hard work starts—not talking. Giving answers and sharing similar experiences ("I know just how you feel. One time I . . . .") are some of the surest ways to short-circuit communication.

Repeating or rephrasing what people say is often helpful in encouraging them to say more. You might say, "You resented what they said," or, "You were hurt by their comments."

Sometimes even repeating outlandish statements in an even tone of voice can help people see what they really mean. For instance, if Jill says, "I just could have killed them for it."

You would respond, "You could have killed them."

Then Jill might say, "Well, I wasn't going to get a gun or anything, but I felt like they broke a promise."

Open-ended questions of how, what, when or where instead of closed-ended questions that can be answered in one word help people gain insight into themselves and their situations. These questions open channels of communication allowing the individual to embellish answers and make a full response. ("When did you start feeling that way?") To listen means to avoid quick answers and easy advice. How often have you heard the words, "Thanks for just listening"?

Just after our first son was born, I became very irritable with Andy. I growled at him for absolutely no reason at all. I felt tense and angry on the inside. I did not know what was bothering me. At lunch Andy asked me a few questions. Finally the problem came out.

I had heard about a mother who had died in childbirth just days after Stephen was born. Her infant son and husband were left without her. I cried and cried as I told Andy about it. I felt great relief in knowing what was bothering me. Talking did not take away the pain. In fact the pain intensified when I became aware of its cause. The thought of that child being separated from his mother was excruciatingly painful. I could not rock and nurse Stephen without weeping for a long time after. But there was great relief in knowing what was bothering me, and my emotional energy could then be directed toward the pain instead of in these other ugly ways.

Another step to effective communication is being an empathic person. Empathy is attempting to see the world through the eyes of others—the capacity to hear with another's ears and respond with another's heart. Empathy is responding "as if" in another's shoes. Touch, tears and silence when appropriate is a part of active listening. Helping people see options for themselves (not telling them what to do) when there appears to be no way out is also empathy.

Empathy, not sympathy is the goal. Sympathy is getting caught up with what *you* feel rather than what the person you are caring for feels. You want to be able to move in someone else's frame of reference without losing your own. You want to provide sensitive objectivity, not lose yourself in unhelpful subjectivity.

I have been in relationships in which I lost objectivity. Though I was supposed to be helping, I got caught up in how *I felt* about how they were doing instead of how the individuals were feeling. Instead of helping them to define and clarify options, I attempted to make their choices for them. The relationships moved from being helpful to creating problems. I had to change and work at again becoming empathic instead of sympathetic.

Communication Barriers

Just as there are steps to communication there are definite barriers against communication. One such barrier is the concept that Christians should not have fears, doubts or be angry with God, or with anyone for that matter It is not easy for us to admit fears, doubts or anger under any circumstances. But when I act like I or other Christians shouldn't have such emotions, it is that much more difficult for those in need to talk about them.

My idea that I needed to protect God's image by acting as if I had no problems, especially with younger Christians, was also a barrier. Finally, I was challenged by one of those "younger Christians" who told me that if I did not begin to share myself with her, she would be more cautious about sharing with me.

Another barrier to communication is feeling defeated or helpless. Talking about victory, success and good feelings is more fun. We often feel like failures when we describe feelings of defeat and helplessness. Yet as I have confessed my sin to others, they have prayed for me and forgiven me as well as communicated God's forgiveness. Growth and change and hope result. Sometimes the growth is agonizingly slow, but it is there, nonetheless. This confession has also bonded me with others who struggle in some of the same ways.

Playing games about issues instead of having open and honest discussion about them is an obvious barrier to effective communication. One game is talking to others about tensions you have with an individual instead of talking directly to that person.

There is also the game of saying that everything is okay when it isn't. Bill suspects Terry is upset with him and asks Terry about it. Terry assures Bill there is no problem but acts in ways that clearly show he is angry. This gives power to Terry, the game player, over Bill who genuinely wants to make things right.

Another game is making people guess your needs. "If they really cared, they'd know I need time alone. I wouldn't have to tell them," we might say. When they don't meet our need, we become angry because "they don't care." But the truth is that often people have no idea what we are thinking unless we tell them. We cannot insist that someone be a mind reader to prove his or her love.

Advice giving is a barrier to communication. Too often quick answers indicate that we aren't really listening and really do not understand. It can make people feel that you would rather give advice than to work at understanding what they are going through. Giving advice often cuts off communication instantly. To help people see their options, on the other hand, is helpful. Our role is not to give advice but to help people decide for themselves what they want to do after they have considered all the possibilities.

Similar to giving advice is telling people they shouldn't feel a certain way ("Now, now, there is no need to take it so hard") or that they don't feel a certain way ("You're not really jealous"). Few responses are more infuriating to a person who is trying to be open. We don't have to approve of what people feel, and it is best to withhold judgment. Nonetheless, we should seek to accept what they say with an understanding ear.

True communication is possible. We can be the Skin Horse for other people. When we can be people who treat others with respect, who don't have to pretend to be real, then through our shabbiness, we have become real ourselves.

Questions for Groups and Individuals

1. How do you identify with the velveteen rabbit?

2. How does this story influence you in your relationships with others?

3. As you think about God as your role model for communication, how would you like to be more like him in the way you communicate with others?

4. With what steps and barriers to communication do you struggle most?

5. How are your communication needs met?

6. What communicates love to you?

7. What happens when your communication needs are not met?

8. What does experiencing "real communication" do for you?

For Further Study:

The Character of Caring People, Resources for Caring People.

5/Caring for Spiritual Needs

I *was back at work after several days off. I received the report about the patients* on the unit and was scurrying around setting up medications before I made my first rounds. I was startled by a crash that came from down the hall out of one of our isolation rooms.

I rushed down to the room. Kathy was sitting on the side of her bed crying. I glanced at the chair that she had thrown against the wall. The telephone was off the hook hanging over her bedside table.

When I sat down beside her and took her hand, she cried out, "I hate my father!" She had been talking to him on the phone and ended the conversation abruptly by hanging up on him.

Kathy was in the hospital with hepatitis caused from taking drugs with contaminated needles. The father that she hated was an alcoholic. Her parents were divorced and her mother was remarried. She had had sexual relationships with several young men. She was nineteen years old and was not in school or able to keep a job.

In the midst of great physical and emotional needs her spiritual needs were evident too. Because she had never known the love of an earthly father, God's love was foreign to her. Yet her sexual life and hatred for her father revealed her craving for love. She had never known what it was to be forgiven. Using drugs and her directionlessness were symptoms of the absence of meaning and purpose in her life.

We are integrated wholes, however. You cannot easily separate physical from emotional from spiritual needs. Kathy was a perfect example of this. Nonetheless, it is helpful to try to look at these different needs separately, especially because spiritual needs can often be at the root of the others.

What Are Our Spiritual Needs?

In *Spiritual Care,* Sharon Fish and Judy Shelly say that for an individual, "a harmonious relationship with himself (characterized by a sense of joy and peace) and rich, meaningful relationships with other people can only be truly experienced when a person first establishes and maintains a dynamic and personal relationship with God who is the key to physical, emotional, social and spiritual integration. A lack of relationship with God can lead to discordant relationships with others.

"The primary reason for this need for a relationship with God lies in the nature of God, who is both personal and dynamic—actively involved in the world he has created. Paul Steeves describes God the Creator as the holy, almighty God who desires to 'enter into direct, intimate, personal relationship with his creatures.'

"God is a father to all people in the sense of giving all people life and breath. But the Fatherhood of God and the resulting benefits of sonship can only be fully realized when a person is able to experience God as the source of meaning and purpose, love and relatedness, and forgiveness. These are three factors which contribute to the establishment and maintenance of a dynamic and personal relationship with God.

"A lack of any one of these three factors will produce a spiritual need, which can be simply defined: *A spiritual need is the lack of any factor or factors necessary to establish and/or maintain a dynamic, personal relationship with God.*

"Because God is the source of these factors, a relationship is established and maintained as an individual responds to God in obedience, according to the grace God has offered. Illness and other forms of crisis can impair a person's ability to sense God's desire for a relationship and can make a person feel hopeless, unloved and unforgiven." We can be the channel to express God's offer of love, meaning and purpose, and forgiveness.

My neighbor, Jo Ann, was scheduled for surgery. She had sporadically come to our neighborhood Bible study. She had been exposed to God's love enough to whet her appetite for a relationship with him. She *thought* she came to our home that day to talk about her upcoming surgery. She really came because she needed to know God. The surgery was a crisis that was the catalyst which brought this spiritual need to the surface.

She responded openly to such questions as "What are you afraid of?" "When you think about God, what do you feel and what do you think?" and "How meaningful is prayer to you?" Soon it became apparent, not only to me, but to her, that her deepest need was spiritual. Jo Ann was seeking to be loved and forgiven. She needed to have some meaning and purpose to her life. She was seeking a relationship with God.

The Need for Meaning and Purpose

Viktor Frankl, a well-known Viennese psychiatrist, writes that a primary force in our life is a search for meaning and purpose. This includes meaning for life in general and meaning in suffering in particular. This need is summarized by Friedrich Nietzsche, a German philosopher. "He who has a *why* to live can bear with almost any *how.*"

However, as we look at the well-known Old Testament character Job, we see that God revealed to him not the *why* but the *who* in life that gives meaning and purpose and therefore hope.

Job was a godly and faithful man. Crisis upon crisis came into his life— the death of his sheep and cattle, his servants and even his ten children. He suffered physically and lost relationships with his friends and wife. He came to the end of himself. He wanted to die and told his "comforters" that given the chance, he'd tell God he didn't deserve this suffering.

Finally God spoke to Job directly. He told Job it was enough to know that God was in control of not only the universe, but his suffering as well. Job needed no further answers. He became secure because his relationship with God was deepened. He knew not the why, but the *who* in a new way.

God offers more to us than just the promise of being in control of the present. God offers us a meaningful and purposeful future by being in control of it too. For those who come to him through his Son, he promises eternal relationship with himself and to end all suffering. Harmonious relationships with God, with ourselves and with others will someday be perfectly and wholly restored.

The Need for Love

Studies have shown that infants will die if they are not held, cuddled, carried and caressed. It is not a luxury for a child to be loved. A child needs touch to survive. This need does not cease to exist when a child becomes an adult. This need for love may in fact intensify—depending on how adequately this need has been met throughout life. Self-pity, insecurity, isolation, desperation and fear are some of the symptoms when this need for love is not met. The loss or absence of human relationship as a primary source of love can contribute to depression or even a desire to die. How we are loved directly affects how we receive God's love and how we love him and each other.

As caring people our goal is to love unconditionally. Such love has no strings attached. This love only wants the person to be open to receive it. This is how God loves. He takes the initiative, but does not force his love on us. Acknowledging and responding to his love draws us into a safe and meaningful love relationship with God. We then can experience self-worth, joy, security, belonging, hope and courage.

"There is no fear in love," says John in his epistle, "but perfect love casts out fear" (1 Jn 4:18). Fish and Shelley have defined fear as "the painful emotion that arises at the thought that we may be harmed or made to suffer and persists while we are subject to the will of someone who does not desire our well-being. The moment we come under the protection of one of good will, fear is cast out."

Need, crisis and illness can intensify fear. As I write, we are in the midst of the war with Iraq. I, like everyone else, have had knots in my stomach. Allied pilots have been taken as prisoners of war with signs that they have received cruel treatment. They are "subject to the will of those who do not desire their well-being." Civilians in Israel, Saudi Arabia and Iraq are being hurt and killed.

On the other hand, when I am aware of God's character (his love and faithfulness), then I can find calm in the midst of the uncertainty and fear.

A knowledge of God's presence is one key to experiencing his love. While the fact of God's control can be a comfort in itself, worshiping a God who desires the best good is equally important to a sufferer.

People who are experiencing God's love are able to see themselves as people of worth. This frees them to love God, themselves and others. You as a caring person are a channel of God's love to others.

The Need for Forgiveness

"I am forgiven" is the liberating message of the gospel. This is the message that we are taking to people we are caring for. It comes as no surprise that the need for forgiveness is one of the basic factors that will produce a spiritual need. Guilt is a very real problem for everyone, whether they are aware of it or not. Forgiveness is not automatically conferred upon people. It is given to those who are willing to receive it. To do so we must confess our rebellion against God, admit our own helplessness and place our faith in Jesus as the only one who is able to save us and restore us to a dynamic, personal relationship with God.

As a caring person, you can become a channel for communicating God's forgiveness as you point the person to Jesus Christ—the source of forgiveness.

The Need for Prayer

Another way to point people to Jesus Christ is by praying with them as well as for them. Praying with someone sets the stage for getting people in touch with God. It allows the opportunity for them to articulate their needs to God. Often the person in need will be unable to pray. You, through the sensitivity of the Holy Spirit, will articulate that person's needs to God.

I met Mr. Lemont while making rounds on the nursing unit. He had just been admitted that afternoon and was scheduled for surgery the next morning. When I walked into his room, he had the curtains pulled around his bed and was sitting quietly in his chair in a dark corner. He didn't say anything. He clasped his hands tightly. His eyes were full of anxiety. I asked him the normal get-acquainted questions like, "Where do you live?" "How many children do you have?" "Grandchildren?"

Though I had just met him, I felt constrained to ask, "Mr. Lemont, are you afraid?" He readily answered yes and seemed relieved to be asked. "What are you afraid of?"

"I am afraid I will not make it through the surgery," he replied as tears came to his eyes.

I took his hand and said, "May I pray with you?"

He squeezed my hand tightly and eagerly said yes.

I thanked God that he was a loving Heavenly Father and the Good Shepherd. I thanked him that he loved Mr. Lemont very much and that he understood his apprehension and promised to go through the surgery with him. I prayed for the doctor and the anesthetist. I asked God to use this situation to draw Mr. Lemont closer to himself.

After we prayed it was like the clouds opened and the sun came out. Mr. Lemont opened his curtain and began interacting with his roommate. He smiled and the smile was real. He was relaxed. He had had an encounter with God.

By coming to God in prayer we are confessing our dependence on God. We are saying that we are not God. When we pray with someone else, we bring that person to the One much greater than us or them—to the One who can meet them in their need. Ultimately prayer is an affirmation of hope.

Principles about Praying

There are no strict rules for when you should pray and when you should not pray with someone—or even how to do it. But there are some general principles.

☐ Remember that prayer is not magical. We do not manipulate God with our prayers. We come to express honestly our needs and desires. We can help people articulate these needs or discover what they are.

☐ Express gratitude, praise and celebration to God. Even in the darkest hour we are coming to a tender, loving and understanding God. Focus on him. Praise him for his character.

☐ Affirm God's presence. The ministry of prayer is the ministry of being there. No matter how grave the circumstances God has not abandoned us. He will walk through the circumstances with us.

Mrs. Smith had been a patient for many days. She had asthma. I walked into her room. She was having difficulty breathing. I took her hand. "Please do not leave me," she said. "Mrs. Smith," I responded, "the time will come that I will have to leave, but I know someone who will never leave you."

We discussed the security in knowing that Jesus would never leave us. We talked about what it meant to come to know Jesus. She prayed with me and asked Jesus to forgive her for her sins and thanked him that he would never leave her.

The art of ministry in prayer is the art of timing. We do not pray because it meets our need "to have prayed with someone." We pray when we are prompted by the Holy Spirit to pray. We pray when the conversation leads to that opportunity or in the presence of anxiety. We pray when people ask us to pray or when we ask them if they want us to pray and they say yes.

Using Scripture

As with prayer so the art of sharing Scripture is an art of timing. If even right answers or right words from Scripture are given at the wrong time, they may not only be unhelpful, but cause pain and damage. Sometimes quoting Scripture can be like giving answers or advice or telling people they shouldn't feel a certain way. This can cut off communication. Sharing Scripture must come after you understand the need of the person you are caring for. It should not come from your need to share Scripture with someone. The hope-giving aspect of Scripture and the role and responsibility of a comforter is described in Isaiah 50:4: "The Lord God has given me the tongue of those who are taught, that I may know how to sustain with a word him that is weary. Morning by morning he wakens, he wakens my ear to hear as those who are taught" (RSV).

I remember when Jody asked, "How do I get to know God?" We looked at the story of Nicodemus in John's Gospel because her questions were like those of Nicodemus. We discussed what it meant to be born into God's family. Jody was ready and became a Christian.

Then there was Tom who was very afraid before going to surgery. We looked at Psalm 23 and shared thoughts about the Lord, our Shepherd, giving us all that we need and going with us through dark valleys. Tom didn't have to be afraid because Jesus his Shepherd was with him. We prayed together.

He seemed to be at peace.

Be Patient

As caregivers we are ambassadors with the message of healing (2 Cor 5:16). This is complex, requiring discernment, sensitivity and a personal prayer life that equips us for such a ministry. But it is made simple by the grace and power of the Lord at work in us and through us as we step out in faith to minister to another. It is the Spirit of God who heals, redeems and offers hope. The following poem by Bonnie Miller summarizes the qualities of God's grace:

God's grace is
—peace in conflict and turmoil.
—courage in fear.
—power in helplessness.
—hope in hopelessness.
—flinchlessness in pain.
—forgiveness in sin.
—vision in frustration.
—tears.
—laughter.
—joy in sorrow.
—self-control in worthlessness.
—wisdom in ignorance.
—feeling loved when I know I'm not lovely.
—comfort when I could scream with pain.
—contentment in waiting when the future is uncertain.
—radiant health though physically limited.
—rejoicing instead of anger.
—unconditional acceptance of myself.
—strength in weakness.
—selecting the right priorities.
—presence in abandonment.
God's grace is the reality of his presence.

Questions for Groups or Individuals

1. What was your definition of spiritual need before you read this chapter? How has that definition been changed or modified?

2. How do you see a personal relationship with God speaking to the need for love, meaning and purpose, and forgiveness?

3. Which of the spiritual needs: love, meaning and purpose, and forgiveness have not been met in your life?

4. How would you say your need for meaning and purpose, love and forgiveness has been met?

5. What helpful and unhelpful responses did you receive from others when you were in spiritual need?

What made the response helpful? Unhelpful?

6. Describe what it was like when you cared for someone who was in spiritual need.

7. Describe a time when you have been ministered to through the use of Scripture and prayer.

For Further Study:

Caring for Spiritual Needs.

6/Caring for People Who Suffer

*A*t times it feels as if even God has forsaken me."

"My fatigue limits me. Physically, emotionally and spiritually, I am often drained by just coping with the basics of living."

"In these times of darkness, a real discouragement, depression and despair hangs heavy over me. I draw further into myself. This strain in my emotions and my body often leave me unable to concentrate for even a few minutes. My thoughts wander and I can't remember or repeat Scripture, pray or have consistent devotional times."

These are just a few of the cries of pain and despair that come from the hearts of people who are suffering. Whether their pleas are silent or spoken, they long for someone to hear what they are trying to say.

Why Do We Suffer?

Different people have different ideas on what the Bible says about suffering. Perhaps that is because Scripture says that suffering may have a number of causes.

Galatians 6:7 says if we sow corruption, we will reap corruption. This suggests that suffering is the result of selecting priorities that can result in illness, physical or emotional pain, or even death.

Suffering can also be spiritual in nature when we refuse to acknowledge or respond to God and his instructions. It is a manifestation of sin which is cured by confession and prayer (Jas 5:13-18). Judgmental attitudes and unchaste behavior can cause broken relationships, harden our hearts toward God, and produce selfishness, jealousy, bitterness and insecurity. Repressing such feelings can bring physical and emotional distress, even damaging illness.

Another cause for suffering according to Paul was his need to not get conceited. Paul struggled with a "thorn in the flesh." He called upon God three times to take it away. Instead of taking it away, God told Paul that he would experience his strength through pain. Paul quit fighting the thorn and began to see it as suffering which would bring him close to God.

Someone else's sin can also cause us suffering. People are often the innocent victims of the evil others create. Rape, robbery or injury from a drunk driver are dramatic examples. Sometimes victims think they brought their problems on themselves. This is often not the case at all. It is very cruel and unChristlike to suggest that if such victims had more faith they would not have problems. Jesus' response to the oppressed was compassion, not condemnation.

When we suffer for doing right, for living like Christians should, the result can be rejection and ridicule (1 Pet 2:18-25). Refusing to go along with the crowd can mean losing friends. Suffering can also come from spreading the good news of Jesus—persecution for the sake of the gospel. Peter learned that godly behavior in suffering wins people to Christ, silences the foolish and ignorant, brings glory to God and makes us Christlike. Righteous people may have many troubles, but the Lord delivers them from them all (34:19).

With this understanding of Scripture, caring people can be more compassionate and open with those who are suffering. Knowing what the Bible says about our own sinful condition should make us less likely to condemn others. Our job is not to pass judgment but to bring God's healing to the hurting.

What Does Suffering Look Like?
There are all kinds of symptoms and behavior that occur when people are suffering. Sufferers can be self-centered or angry or bitter or complaining or have frequent mood swings. They may make great demands of God—such

as restoring what they've lost. They may cry, or they may be stoic. They may pray more genuinely than ever or stop praying altogether. They may see God's grace more clearly while they suffer, or they may have serious doubts about whether God even exists. They may even exhibit all of these behaviors at different times.

Understanding the difference between *acute* and *chronic* suffering can help us know how to help people better. Almost any kind of suffering will fall under one of these two categories, whether it is physical, spiritual, emotional or psychological.

Acute suffering usually comes suddenly, is short-term (relatively speaking), is intense in symptoms, and often demands immediate and urgent attention and care. A heart attack is an obvious example of an acute physical illness. One kind of acute emotional illness occurs when strong and conflicting emotions intensify to the point that a person "breaks" (that is, cannot continue to function) or feels like he or she will "break" under the stress.

The treatment of someone who is suffering from an acute illness requires only short-term lifestyle changes. If a child has been in a car accident, family members will cancel their immediate plans to be in the hospital. They (as well as the victim) are likely to experience shock and great anxiety because the trauma was so sudden, severe and completely unexpected. They will need physical, emotional, spiritual and financial resources immediately. Frequent visits, phone calls, cards and tokens of care (flowers, meals, and so on) can meet many of these needs.

Because acute suffering is short, people can sometimes cover up their deep anxiety. But the pain is still there and eventually will need care. This care is especially necessary if the acute condition is very serious or life-threatening in nature. If it results in death, there often is no time for the sufferer to conclude unfinished business—say good-by, ask forgiveness, or tell someone, "I love you."

Chronic suffering on the other hand may develop slowly, last a long time and recur frequently. A chronic disease is one that is always present, constantly weakening, vexing or troubling the sufferer.

Chronic suffering requires both long-term and short-term action. Often the family and the individual need to make permanent changes in lifestyle. When long-term care is needed, too often the person is forgotten by others. Anger, fear and loneliness can also be more intense than with acute suffering.

Chronic sufferers desperately need a sense of hope and purpose. Families can find the situation very wearing and financially draining over the long haul. Maintaining a façade is much more difficult during this type of suffering. Depending on the condition, the person may have to constantly prepare for more loss of health—and even death. When death follows a long illness, the family has probably done a good deal of grieving during the illness.

"My sense of self-worth and dignity as a person is being jeopardized," says Terry. "My body itself is in such a process of change, as is my lifestyle. I hardly feel I know myself from day to day. This makes me insecure and frightened."

Bill put it this way: "I feel enraged at times for my body betraying me, and for the pain and my diminished and unpredictable energy level. I feel undependable and afraid to make commitments."

"My feelings of helplessness often engulf me and bring near panic," said Chris. "I feel useless and cut off from the mainstream of full, productive life. I feel like I am nothing. I have never felt like I was valued or worthwhile."

"People are busy and proud of it," noted Joyce. "It seems so 'spiritual' to be doing. Even the Christian world doesn't seem to affirm my value or worth in some quiet service."

How Can I Help?

To be used by God to care for those who are suffering is a great privilege. God offers to them his love and comfort. He promises to provide for their daily needs. He accepts them when their behavior is difficult to accept. He even promises, "My grace is sufficient for you, for my power is made perfect in weakness" (2 Cor 12:9). As his followers he has chosen to allow us to be both recipients and transmitters of that wonderful grace to others.

The following are some key principles which will help you to care for those who are suffering:

Know yourself. You must begin the process of thinking through and looking at how you are affected by suffering and death. You need to come to terms with your own death. Otherwise, it is very difficult to effectively care for someone who is suffering or dying.

This doesn't mean you have to have all the answers. No one really can explain death. But if you avoid talking about death because of fear and uncertainty, you will not allow others to talk about their death—which they very much need to do.

To know yourself is also to know your limitations. It is very hard for me to say, "I cannot do it." But I have failed a lot lately precisely because I have pushed beyond my limits. I have learned to say such things as, "I cannot help you with this because I have lost all objectivity." That has freed me enough to direct that person to someone else for help.

Learn to love unconditionally. Many times we experience great satisfaction in caring for others. People grow, are healed, change and sometimes even appreciate what we have done for them. But at other times none of this happens. Still we are called on to love and to do what is right even if the results aren't visible—even for a long time. We need eyes to see that others are in process. This usually does not happen until we can see that we ourselves are in process.

Learn to see what is not expressed, and hear what is not spoken. We live in a world in which people hide behind all kinds of masks. There is the "I'm fine" mask, or the "I do not need anyone" mask. People are afraid to really talk about how they are feeling. They have been hurt by others and do not want to be hurt again.

It is important to observe body language (for example, arms folded across the chest can mean defensiveness), facial expressions (wandering eyes could mean fear or lack of concentration), and posture (slouching can mean defiance or depression). Such clues can help us to not assume that the person is all right.

Know helpful communication skills. Facilitating communication with someone in need is a great gift to that person. Communication is an agent of growth and healing. (More is said about this in chapter five.) To become skilled in asking questions and communicating with others is a high and worthwhile goal. Genuine care for that person is what motivates our communicating with them.

Often when people think of communication they think of talking. But listening is the most important ingredient in good communication, not talking. Becoming an active listener is of vital importance for the caring person.

Give the gift of encouragement. One of the most effective ways of affirming someone is by listening to that person. A person who is listened to feels loved, valued and important. There are many other ways to encourage others, such as giving compliments and saying thank you. We should be asking ourselves on a regular basis, "What can I say or do to encourage this person?"

Learn the ministry of your presence. Just as we are confident that we will not be abandoned by God, people who are hurting need that same assurance that we will not abandon them. Especially in this culture where so many are screaming "me first," one of the most valuable gifts you can give to someone is to lay aside your own interests and spend time with that person. The ministry of presence is the ministry of love.

Learn to receive. A sign of accepting ourselves is the ability to be open about our own needs and failures. We need help from others. People often resist relationships that are one-sided, in which one person does all the receiving and is not allowed to give. It is tempting for people who give all the time to act like what is given to them is not adequate or helpful. The truth is that we are all in desperate need of the grace of God. It is dishonest to pretend that we are not.

Learn to wait on the Lord. Discouragement can come to those who are caregivers. Our involvement in another's life can seem to be making no difference. We are tempted to lose heart. That is the time to wait on God. Waiting means having hope, being patient, not expecting or being disappointed if there are not immediate results. Waiting on God is acknowledging that he is the one who must do the healing. I cannot. I will wait to see what he will do.

Learn to expect results from the power of the Word and prayer. Scripture and prayer are great resources in the hands of those who are ministering to others. However, I must be first experiencing the healing and power of Scripture and prayer before I can expect to see it effective in the lives of others. I need the nurture and strength and renewal which comes from times with God.

Develop support systems to strengthen your ministry. I confess sin, share needs, am prayed for and am encouraged within the Christian community. In the context of a support system I change and grow and experience God's grace through others. Those I am caring for will be prayed for by people who love me. Those who are suffering and those who do not know God will be able to see him better by being exposed to other Christians.

Be purposeful and timely. Even Jesus did not meet all the needs of all that he encountered. He was in tune with his Father and did his Father's will. As we are people of prayer and the Scripture in the context of Christian community, we gain a sense of God's purposes and priorities by which to live and minister.

Talking about suffering in general terms is difficult to do. Each person who suffers is unique and each kind of suffering is unique to that person—though others may have faced similar types of pain. Don't feel the need to apply all of these principles all at once. Find the one that best fits the individuals you are caring for and seek to develop it as a means of grace to them.

Questions for Groups or Individuals

1. What is your understanding of acute and chronic suffering?
2. Give examples of both acute and chronic illness that you have observed.
3. What has been your personal experience with suffering and pain?
4. How do you feel when you observe another's discomfort?
5. How do you usually respond to suffering?
6. Principles of caring for those who suffer are discussed in this chapter. Which seem most difficult and which seem least difficult? Why?

For Further Study:

Caring for Physical Needs, Caring for Emotional Needs, Caring for Spiritual Needs.

7/Caring for People in Crisis

L ife in the fast lane. *Worries about financial investments and stock-market highs and lows. No time for leisure. Family gets pushed to the side. No time for relationships. No time to nurture the spirit or the soul.* Then, one day the bottom falls out.

The climb up the corporate ladder yields only frustration, loneliness, brokenness, high blood pressure, high cholesterol and spiritual bankruptcy.

Health-care professionals establishing a practice, hard-working young students, as well as business people working their way up corporate ladders while raising a family all face these same crushing pressures and inevitable human responses.

Many people who are functional in their day-to-day responsibilities are also experiencing the pain of emotional distancing and physical illness. They are ripe for a crisis. Anything could tip the scales, disorganize their schedules and force them to learn to use new coping mechanisms—or to discover firsthand the reality of being mortal.

Distorted Images of God
Everyone experiences stress-producing situations that threaten to take them beyond their ability to cope. Hanging on to the reality of a loving Father, a redeeming Savior and an intervening Holy Spirit when spiritual nurturing has

long been forgotten is extremely difficult. Even when individuals *have* taken great pains to nurture the spiritual aspects of life, a crisis can shake the very foundations of their ability to maintain that faith and the courage to survive.

Misconceptions about God can make a crisis even more difficult by driving us from him, rather than to him. Sarah, a 28-year-old mother of two toddlers and the wife of a busy salesman, was hospitalized for arthritis. Sarah had never had symptoms of this disease until three weeks earlier. Now, she could not walk, or carry or care for the children. The acute stress of this situation generated extreme fear and hopelessness. While talking with her nurse, she said that she believed God was punishing her because her three-year-old son had been born before she was married. She believed she had transgressed God's law so badly that he could not forgive her for that and now he was punishing her.

Sam has similar misbeliefs about God. Sam's son just told him that he is gay. Sam does not understand why God is punishing him in this way. He says that he has been "good all his life," and he doesn't deserve this. Therefore, God must be capricious and unjust.

These perceptions of God are inaccurate and contribute to the stressful responses of these individuals to their crises. Both individuals are looking for meaning in what they are experiencing. Both individuals are attempting to cope with crisis and its resulting pain and fear.

Responding to Crisis

When confronted with a situation or incident that threatens to take us out of control, to disorganize our "normal" patterns or response, all of us go through a series of contrasting responses. These responses have been called the "Dramas of Crisis" (Nighswonger, 1971). They consist of a series of events having dramatic unity and interest, usually vivid and moving. Though at times we consider such dramas to reflect anticipation of physical death, remember, life is full of deathlike experiences all of which create these dramas in our lives in varying degrees.

Christians and non-Christians alike will experience these dramas as they work at finding meaning in difficult situations. Families and friends who observe such dramas in their loved ones may also experience the same dramas. The dramas are necessary and important to experience as part of the growing, healing process of learning to cope and learning to hope.

Briefly, the dramas of crisis are:

(1) The Drama of Shock: Denial versus Panic

(2) The Drama of Emotion: Catharsis versus Depression

(3) The Drama of Negotiation: Bargaining versus Selling Out

(4) The Drama of Cognition: Realistic Hope versus Despair

(5) The Drama of Commitment: Acceptance versus Resignation

(6) The Drama of Completion: Fulfillment versus Forlornness

The *drama of shock* is the stunned response to receiving the news of something threatening—illness, business collapse, impending divorce, death. This drama is marked by denial and panic.

Denial is the emotional shock absorber that allows us to pretend we did not hear that which we cannot emotionally accept. Denial provides what can be called a "psychic anesthetic" to an otherwise unbearable reality. This type of response is considered to be normal and healthy because it gives people time to muster their inner resources to cope with the situation. Prolonged denial, however, indicates an inability to deal with the drama and prevents the person from seeking further treatment.

Panic, the alternate response to denial, is rarely found to be constructive. The reality of the situation produces terror in the individual to the point of generating impulsive, uncontrolled and unrealistic behavior. The goal becomes escaping the situation no matter what the cost, even if it means the taking of their own life.

The *drama of emotion* follows when reality sets in. The individual begins to express the flood of emotions either through catharsis (openly talking about feelings) or turning these emotions inward—which produces depression.

When feelings are openly expressed, there is usually a flood of anger characterized by the searching question "Why me?" There is at the core of that question the flavor of the unfairness of it all. Helpers often find the anger directed at them as representatives of God.

The greatest help to someone struggling through these emotions is your willingness to listen, love and accept. Recognize that you cannot answer the question "Why me?" In reality, people in crisis do not expect you to answer the question, but they need to be free to ask it without condemnation. They also need the freedom to be angry, without being judged by the helper.

God is not offended by the anger of a person in crisis. He knows those cries are the painful cries for help and healing. They are cries for his presence and intervention. That's where you come in. You can represent God's presence as kind, compassionate, gentle, understanding and powerful. This is a tremendous challenge to our faith and our mission which we are not capable of taking on by ourselves, but the Spirit is fully capable of empowering us to meet the challenge.

Depression is the result of not being able or allowed to experience catharsis, causing the resolution of the conflict of this drama to go unresolved. Well-meaning friends and relatives may create this problem by telling the people in crisis that they "shouldn't feel that way," or "Christians shouldn't get angry because God has everything under control." However, when kept from expressing negative feelings, people may turn their feelings inward, developing a deep sense of guilt and shame which can reach neurotic proportions.

The *drama of negotiation* is characterized by the "let's make a deal" attitude. The individual in crisis is looking for a way out. If the intensity of the guilt and shame in depression is not resolved, selling out becomes the only "deal" that is made. The "what's the use?" attitude is the hallmark of unresolved depression. People must be encouraged to talk about the feelings that led to this point of personal and spiritual bankruptcy.

The better place for people to be in working out what has happened to them is to be bargaining or contemplating a "deal" that says "maybe not me." The "deal" might be with the doctor or the nurses, the alienated spouse, or a new drug treatment program. The hope is that something, someone—perhaps the one in crisis—can make a change that will alter the outcome in a more positive direction.

The *drama of cognition* is characterized by recognition of the reality of a given situation as perhaps inalterable. The concern now is to find meaning in it all. The alternatives in the drama are hope or despair.

Individuals can be helped through their experiences to find meaning and purpose in their pilgrimages which, even in the face of death, will offer personal fulfillment. As a result, spiritual attitudes and a deeper understanding of biblical truths become more evident. Anger will give way to receiving encouragement and hope from God. Questions of eternal destiny and a refining of our perspective on life are expressed in an effort to find ultimate meanings to experience.

People who have experienced spiritual and personal bankruptcy, on the other hand, have no sense of hope, finding no meaning in life's experiences. These individuals become bitter and gloomy. Such despair is the result of emptiness, the feeling of being unworthy, "bad," unloved, unheard, unaccepted.

Even at this point, there is no need for the helper to despair for our Lord will show this individual his love, his compassion, his acceptance. Be careful to affirm the value of the individual but also take care not to offer them a superficial fix, or a Christ who is not hearing them or attending to their cries.

The *drama of commitment* is often difficult to distinguish as the person moves from developing that realistic sense of hope to acceptance. Likewise, movement from despair to resignation is also difficult to discern. The shift in these emotions generally comes when the individual has moved from intellectual assent to emotional response.

Either hope is affirmed with the confidence and assurance that meaning will be experienced, or resignation results from the sense of despair. Resignation is the result of a pilgrimage that spiritually ended in the third drama. Having sold out, the individual is resigned to inevitable meaninglessness. Hope, however, gives people the courage to be, to more fully internalize their faith, to find the connection between what they believe about life and death and how it feels living with or through the present crisis.

The *drama of completion* in the pilgrimage through crisis is characterized by fulfillment or forlornness.

The forlorn traveler withdraws feeling abandoned, forsaken and despairing. The suffering is not ignored but the individual finds no peace and longs for death with almost a bitter rage. Those called upon to help the forlorn often become bewildered, frustrated and fearful. The possibility of reversing these emotional responses seems impossible. Apart from the powerful intervention of Christ and the consistent presence and compassion of those in the helping role, such people are lost in their aloneness. Though in human terms this condition appears impossible to reverse, the Lord Christ longs to intervene and give comfort and healing of spirit and soul—perhaps even physical healing. Some, however, may never experience this healing.

Fulfillment stands in contrast to the emotional response of forlornness. Fulfillment allows the sufferer to stand in peace and tranquillity with dignity while the waters around them are turbulent and fierce. The person in crisis has grasped the precious reality of the constancy of the Father, the redemption of the Son, and indwelling courage of the Holy Spirit that provide meaning and purpose and unshakable peace until full resolution comes.

Waiting It Out

Caring for people in crisis is demanding and often shakes the helper's faith as the realization comes that often there are no answers, only questions, or that offers of comfort are batted away leaving the helper to feel inadequate and insensitive.

The true sufferer experiences extremely intense and often unremitting emotional, spiritual and physical pain. The experience requires that the individual go it alone. No other person can fully know the extent of their pain. But the helper's willingness to know helps to relieve some of the intensity of the suffering, it dissipates the intensity of the aloneness, helps to reorganize perceptions and thought patterns, gives hope.

Your greatest equipment in serving others in crisis is your patient and perceptive ears and eyes, and sometimes your touch. Through your sensitivity to God's Spirit, you are able to bring to others God's healing and forgiving grace. Your readiness to intervene in this way depends on your own willingness to be vulnerable, available and open through your relationship with Christ and the indwelling of his Spirit.

Many times the question is asked, "How long does it take for a person to experience all of this?" That is personal and highly dependent on two factors: the personal reserves from making it through past crises successfully and the availability of someone walking with them through the experience. A rough estimate, however, in weeks and months is anywhere from six weeks to twelve months.

The helper's ability to "hang in there" during those long months of crisis is vital, providing the most unique and deeply blessed experience ever known. And the Lord will show you great and mighty things that you do not now know (Jer 33:3).

Questions for Groups or Individuals

1. In anticipating your ministry to people in crisis, in what areas will you need to develop depth of understanding?

2. How will you begin to do that? (Make specific plans.)

3. Given your own faith and personal values, what is your understanding of the significance of life's crises?

4. How will your understanding of crisis help you in ministering to others?

5. Think about the six dramas of crisis. Describe how you have recognized people acting in different stages of the drama of crisis.

6. Think about a specific crisis you saw a friend or relative go through. Given what you have learned in this chapter, how are you better able to help that person now?

7. How does knowing these dramas help you in making yourself vulnerable and available?

8. Have you ever gotten caught up in the dramas of crisis on another person's behalf? Describe what happened.

For Further Study:

Caring for People in Grief, Caring for Emotional Needs.

8/Caring for People in Grief

My husband Andy's mother was a vibrant and youthful seventy-two-year-old. During the last couple years of her life, there were symptoms that indicated that she was not feeling well. She saw a doctor and was diagnosed and scheduled for surgery. We all anticipated that surgery would bring back her health and vitality. Instead, it took her life.

A few days after her death, I was rocking our infant son in her living room. My eyes were fixed on the four portraits that hung on the wall—probably not unlike the way I gazed at them the first time I saw them. They had captivated my heart. Of all the material possessions in this home, the portraits were what I loved most.

Each portrait was of a beautiful three-year-old child. The oldest, Lucy Rae, died of polio as a seven-year-old. This reminded me of the time when I was doing dishes with Andy's mom, and I began asking her about Lucy Rae. Her blue eyes filled with tears as she spoke of her.

As I continued to rock, Andy's sister, who had been packing, came into the room and took her portrait off the wall. It would be going to her home in D.C. In a few minutes John came from the other side of the house and took the portrait of him and the one of his sister, Lucy Rae (John's daughter was named after her and the portrait was his) off the wall. He would take them to their home in Iowa.

Now only Andy's was left. Soon we would be removing it from the wall to take it to our home.

The portraits were separated for the first time in thirty years. They represented the family, who in a more definite sense were going their separate ways. This home—a center for being together—would be no more. The parents, around whom the relationships between the kids revolved, were gone. My grief and feelings of separation were amplified.

Experiencing Grief

Grief is a life-shaking sorrow over loss. It is a complex of emotions we experience when we lose something that we value. Such things as loss of interest in life, mental and emotional pain, loss of appetite and loss of sleep characterize grief. It is full of anxiety and uncertainty. C. S. Lewis wrote that he was surprised at how much grief felt like fear.

Death is the most obvious cause for grief. But there are many other reasons for grieving. Losses in our lives need to be acknowledged and grieved for. For example, some of these losses are divorce, loss of a job, a home taken away, disfiguring surgery, or loss of a limb. All losses are deathlike experiences. Tears are a natural way to express grief. A certain amount of tears need to be shed for each loss. When we tell a person to quit crying we delay the expression of their grief. "Blessed are those who mourn," the Scriptures say, "for they shall be comforted."

Jesus wept when he heard about the death of his friend Lazarus. Tears are healing. They are not a sign of lack of faith nor of hopelessness. Crying should not require an apology or an explanation. Tears wash away the dark tensions of our souls.

Allowing tears to come is difficult because in our culture expressions of grief are often viewed as "bad taste." The normal response to expressions of grief is to give sedatives, or run in and out of people's lives, rather then to sit with people and allow them to cry. And when people do cry it is called "falling apart," "breaking down," or "going to pieces."

Grief work needs to be done and will be done sooner or later. How completely or incompletely depends on how the person is allowed to move through the process of grieving. Grieving must be done before returning to normal activity and emotional stability. When people deny the emotional importance of mourning and try to get on with living without the burden of grieving, severe psychological and psychosomatic illnesses develop.

Silent Comfort

The greatest gift that we have to offer someone who is grieving is our presence. Often that means sitting with them in silence. Letting them talk whenever they want to. Listening to the same story over and over again. Absorbing their pain. Allowing their tears to flow. Weeping with them.

Joe Bayly, in his book *The View from a Hearse,* describes his feelings after the death of one of his sons. "I was sitting, torn by grief. Someone came and talked to me of God's dealings, of why it happened, of hope beyond the grave. He talked constantly, he said things I knew were true.

"I was unmoved, except to wish he'd go away. Finally he did.

"Another came and sat beside me. He didn't talk. He didn't ask leading questions. He just sat beside me for an hour and more, listened when I said something, answered briefly, prayed simply, left.

"I was moved. I was comforted. I hated to see him go."

The one who comforts accepts expressions of grief without judgement. This means not having answers and allowing free expression of feelings. We do not have to defend God. He understands grief as no one else does and he is loving them beyond words.

We live in a death-denying culture. Too often the person who is supposed to comfort avoids talking about death. Usually death is all that the person who is grieving wants to talk about. But people grieving will not talk about death when they sense the caregiver is not comfortable discussing it. In order to effectively offer the gift of my presence to someone else, I have to come to terms with my own death, loss and grief. If I am not at peace in the presence of death, I cannot help someone else to be at peace in the midst of it.

Fear causes us to deny death because the very fact of death brings into question the meaning of life. For instance, "Why was I born?" And of course the question is asked, "What will happen to me after I die?" We are told in Hebrews that the human race is being held in bondage throughout life by the fear of death. But Jesus became like us and by his death freed us from this slavery to the fear of death (Heb 2:14-15).

The person who is grieving may not be able to "feel" God's presence and care. Even as Jesus was God Incarnate, in a sense we are Jesus Incarnate. We are his flesh-and-blood representative to them. Because Jesus' life is in us, if he is our Lord and our Savior, when I share myself with others, I share Jesus with them. My presence with them is Jesus' presence with them.

Practical Help

There are practical things we can do. For instance, at times grieving people will *need* to keep fairly busy. Do not take away all of a person's responsibilities, but rather help as needed. At times people will not be able to function at all and will need everything done for them—meals prepared, bathrooms cleaned, dishes done and children taken care of.

Evenings are often the most lonely times for those who are grieving. Phone calls and visits at this time are usually welcomed.

Mary Jane's husband was killed in a car accident. For several days immediately after Jim's death a friend followed her around with a notebook and pen in hand. This friend kept a running list of all that needed to be done and thought about. Mary Jane said that was one of the most helpful things done for her during that time.

Children must not be forgotten. A grieving parent may not be able to handle the practical aspects of childcare at this time. The children will have spiritual and emotional needs that will demand your attention. A response to their grief, questions, fears, and sense of abandonment by parents who are unable to meet their needs is vital. Children may also be dealing with feelings of guilt and anger, especially if there has been a divorce.

Communicating to People in Grief

We have a very important message to give to grieving people. The feelings and behavior that they are experiencing are normal. It will come to an end. And though life will never be the same without the lost person, relationship, or object, they will, in time resume normalcy.

Grief may need to include forgiveness. Often people need to forgive themselves. Regrets overwhelm those left behind after the death of a loved one. Thoughts of I-did-do-that-I-should-not-have-done or what-I-did-not-do-that-

I-should-have-done can plague a grieving person incessantly.

Sometimes people in grief need to forgive the deceased person or the person who caused the loss (for instance, in a divorce). If this forgiveness is not granted, it is an excellent opportunity for bitterness to set in and to become the focus in this person's life. Grieving people may also need help in working through their angry feelings toward God.

Relief *may* come as you listen and accept their feelings. But the time may come when listening is not enough. I cannot stress the "may come" enough. Nor can I overstress the "might" in the next statement: You *might* need to ask questions to help people in grief to think through their relationships with others and with God. They may need to hear that you do not know the reasons for their loss but that God does. And they need to know that God has not lost control or abandoned them. Most of the time when people who are grieving ask "Why" they are not looking for answers. They simply need to be reminded of God's love. Better yet, they simply need to see that love lived out through us.

Gently reading portions of Scripture can be healing. Grieving people should be encouraged to talk to God about their feelings. There may be times to sensitively share our faith in Jesus Christ.

The Process of Grief

It takes a long, long time to grieve. And it takes a long, long time for the relationship with God to *feel* the way the person thinks it should feel—or for it to be what you, the caregiver, thinks it should be. Time for healing needs to be granted. Do not attempt to rush this process. Do not ask questions too soon or talk too much. Keep talking to a minimum. Listen to the maximum—and then listen some more.

When the cause of grief is death, people spend a great deal of time concentrating on reviewing the details of important past events with the deceased. "In each of these life segments he has to realize afresh the pain of his loss and rather concretely experience its permanence" (Gerald Chaplan). The most intense and lonely time of grief is when the person finally breaks ties with the lost person or object. During this time, people need much support. They will go over and over their image of the person in order to recognize just how much their lives will be affected by the loss. If you knew the deceased, share with the griever how that person had significance in your life. Allow others to share the pain. Try to mobilize supportive people from their church, friends and family.

Throughout the whole process caring people should encourage, touch and show affection to those working through the grief. During grief priorities have a tendency to get shifted. When the loss occurs, it suddenly becomes "me first," then others and then God. People may need help in getting their priorities in order again.

Once the grief work is done and the loss is faced they are ready to begin life again without that which they have lost. This process can take a year or longer. New patterns of living are established. Lifestyle changes are made in accordance with the loss they have faced. They can even begin to reach out to others.

Martin Luther once said, "Until a person experiences suffering he cannot know what it is to hope." We do have great hope because we are Christians! Because Christ lives, we live. Life can be meaningful again. Yes, we grieve. We grieve deeply. This grieving, however, is different than for those who have no hope.

Death is a terrible enemy, but it is an enemy that will be completely destroyed someday. All the other losses that we face can take on their proper perspective in light of the cross of Jesus Christ and our relationship with him. People who have faith have opportunity to give evidence of uncommon relationship with God in times of loss. We come out of grieving as different people. This hope makes it possible to live again!

I close with an excerpt from a Christmas letter in which my friend April articulately communicates her family's experience of loss and grief and hope:

"I've always loved Christmas. It sets my mind spinning with images. Sight, smells and especially sounds (Carols!) pull me fully into celebration. So why, this year, do I cry when I hear the soaring words 'surely He taught us to love one another, His law is love and His Gospel is peace' and 'then pealed the bells more loud and deep, "God is not dead nor dost He sleep, the wrong shall fail, the right prevail, with peace on earth good will toward men?" '

"The tears this year at Christmas are tears of grief that two names we believed would be linked together forever are divorced (a *hard* word). The tears are for grief and for memories on our daughter and her now former husband.

"Sometimes driving home at night from work my eyes are drawn to the startling orange-red beauty of the evening sunset. Nearby the earth-floor is littered with garbage—society's careless litter marring the landscape. Homely drive-ins, architectural travesties impinge upon limited space. Billboard advertisements arch garishly, grabbing our senses for what we do not want or need. Above and beyond it all, at the edge of the world it seems, trunks and branches of black, silhouetted winter trees continue to reach up and up. I feel like a tree, too, feet rooted, arms flung up, eyes lifted above to the amazingly beautiful sky. And I know, again, some of the Promise. It's beginning to come back . . . to settle in my heart. Cold tentacles of sadness or anger or fear reach down less often into simple, happy times.

"But we, my husband, myself and our family, are a part of the brokenness, the litter, the trying pain of the earth-floor as never before. Because we've lost someone. Someone is gone . . . gone from us in all the ways we've known (and fifteen years of knowing is a lot of years. And fifteen years of loving is a lot of years). And our granddaughter's face is too sad for words (sometimes), and her younger sister doesn't know at all yet and that's heartbreaking too, and our daughter is one of our dearest treasures, and we never wanted this for her.

"So we all face this season with memories that are joltingly real. At the same time nothing will ever be the same, some Great Truths are endlessly the same and their verity is like a balm. Oswald Chambers said, 'If God has made your cup sweet drink it with grace; if He has made it bitter, drink it in communion with Him.' So we're learning joy can be had . . . that we're grateful even. That family love and support has never been stronger, that intimacy with each other is rich in both family and friends, that shared brokenness is a privilege. That God is with us (Love came down). And joy is more recognizable, perhaps? (has more clarity?)

"We are thankful for the joy of straight gazes and honest questions that imply Rocklike support—for exquisite truths, ageless, powerful, in spite of circumstance."

April, Bob and their family are coming out of grief as different people.

Questions for Groups or Individuals

1. How have your thoughts about grief been affected by this chapter?

2. How do you think our culture responds to grief and death?

3. When have you observed or been involved with someone who was grieving?

What was it like?

4. When have you experienced grief because of a significant loss?

What was it like?

5. What can you do to begin to come to terms with your own death?

6. What kinds of needs do you think a child would have who lost a parent and/or a sibling through death or divorce?

7. How does your hope in Christ affect the way you think about loss and death?

8. This chapter states that "we come out of grieving as different people." How have you found this to be true?

For Further Study:

Caring for People in Grief.

9/Letting God Care for Us

I t was a cold snowy night and it was a pleasure to be inside, drinking coffee with people we enjoyed. The warmth in our home was made warmer by the stimulating turn in our conversation.

We were meeting with two other couples to plan a retreat for our adult Sunday-school class. At that time we attended a mainline-denomination church. A lot of people in that church had not yet made a personal commitment to Christ. This Sunday-school class had grown from a handful to about forty people.

The planning was done. The pie and ice cream were served. Fork in hand, Michael, the program chairman for the retreat, turned to John, the president of the class, and said, "I know why I haven't become a Christian. But why haven't you?" Michael's tone was as matter-of-fact as if he were asking, "How was your day?" or "What do think about the president's relationship with Congress?"

Smiling on the inside and waiting eagerly for John's response, I thought with glee, "We're supposed to be asking that kind of question. We're the Christians here!" Andy and I glanced at each other. The conversation that was unfolding right in front of our eyes was a wonderful answer to our prayers for these friends.

John replied: "For forty years I have been taught to take care of myself. No one else will do it for me. Now I am hearing in our Bible study that I am supposed to turn everything over to God. How do you expect me to undo what I've learned all my life?"

"My reason for not becoming a Christian," said Michael, "is similar to yours, John. I do not want anyone else to control my life. I want to be in control."

The Problem

Long before Michael or John or any of us wanted to be in control, the problem began. It began in the Garden of Eden with God, Adam and Eve. The three of them were at peace with each other and with the world. Adam and Eve were perfectly comfortable in allowing God to care for them. He provided all that they needed.

Then the serpent came along. His challenge to "be like God" was more than they could resist. Adam and Eve ate of the fruit and immediately began taking care of themselves.

We have been struggling with this "God complex" every since. We will take care of ourselves. We will take care of other people. We will be in control. What we really mean is "We will be like God."

As we strive to be the caring people that God wants us to be, the "god-complex" that we have inherited begins to emerge. Even those of us who have been followers of Jesus much of our lives, who supposedly have "turned everything over to God" already, struggle to allow God to care for us. In the flurry of our lives we make decisions about cars and jobs and churches and trips—and it all rapidly goes by with perhaps only a passing consultation with God. Prayer, which is supposed to indicate our dependence on God, is crushed out of our schedules as we often manage to live our lives quite well without him.

Others of us do not allow God to take care of us because we are too busy taking care of others. Even though male-female roles are changing, we still see a drivenness to care for others more often in women. Our culture has conditioned women to be responsible for taking care of everyone—our children, our husbands, our neighbors, our elderly parents—everyone. Men, of course, can fall into this trap as well.

Being responsible people is fine, but sometimes we are inappropriately responsible. Responsibility is out-of-hand when we take on the needs of the world and neglect caring for ourselves. We can even feel guilty for paying attention to our own concerns. Too often we've heard that the way to "JOY" is putting "Jesus" first, "Others" second and "Yourself" last. But too often that turns into considering yourself not at all.

It is in the midst of our stubbornly saying, "I want to take care of myself," or of our compulsively saying, "I must take care of others," that God lovingly comes to express his love and care for us. It is not easy to let God do this. However, if we do not receive God's care, our care for others will dry up. We will also be cheating ourselves of that wonderful and intimate relationship in which our loving heavenly Father is able to freely express his care for us.

I remember a time when I felt very empty. In tears I talked with Andy. I was not caring for others as I thought I should. My heart did not feel tender. It seemed like everything I did hurt the people I was trying to love. Besides that, I felt like I was not growing spiritually. Though my goal for the year was to grow as a person of prayer, my prayer life was at an all-time low.

Andy listened carefully and then said gently: "You are in a good place before God. You are at a point where you must let him care for you. And that is what he wants to do. You cannot take care of yourself."

Learn to Relax
There are practical ways in which we can let God care for us. The first is simply giving ourselves permission to relax. How? Decide to just sit with a cup of coffee (or tea—not to discriminate against tea drinkers) and watch the beauty of the snowfall. Have popcorn and a Coke with friends with no other purpose in mind than to enjoy them. Laugh—I have friends who renew me because they make me laugh. Rent a video—this is something I had to learn. I enjoy movies but I never had the time to see them because I had too many important things to do. It has helped me to know that it is okay to relax and watch a movie.

These kinds of refreshment are vital. We are driven, goal-oriented and busy all the time. We act as though there is much in life that God cannot handle without us. When we relax, we make a statement about God and we make a statement about ourselves. We are saying that God is God and I am not.

Even when we are not working, God is. God can continue doing his work quite well without us.

Even the great leader of the Reformation, Martin Luther, knew the value of relaxing. He once said, "I sit here and drink my Wittenberg beer, and the gospel runs its course." My intent here is not to endorse Luther's habit of beer drinking, but to show that even this man in whom so much of God's work centered knew that it didn't depend on him. He could relax a bit and the great work of salvation would go on without him.

Give yourself the time and means to relax.

Another way to relax is to take the sabbath seriously. When we do so, we are stating by our lifestyle that God has everything under control. Eugene Peterson, in his article "The Pastor's Sabbath" (*Leadership,* Spring 1985), says: "Sabbath means quit. Stop. Take a break. The word itself has nothing devout or holy in it. It is a word about time, denoting our non-use thereof, what we usually call wasting time. Sabbath keeping is not devout thoughts or heart praise but simply removing ourselves from circulation one day a week."

Peterson claims that "every profession has sins to which it is especially liable." The pastor's sin (and I believe that of the caregiver), he says, is "reversing the rhythms."

Instead of grace/work we make it work/grace. Instead of working in a world in which God calls everything into being with his word and redeems his people with an outstretched arm, we rearrange it as a world in which we preach the mighty work of God and in afterthought ask him to bless our speaking; a world in which we stretch out our mighty arms to help the oppressed and open our hands to assist the needy and desperately petition God to take care of those we miss.

The benefits of rest to our work will be great as well. In "Desert and Harvest: A Sabbatical Journey" (*Leadership,* Winter 1988) Eugene Peterson reports the benefits of his sabbatical year:

Everything I hoped for came to pass: I returned with more energy than I can remember having since I was fifteen years old. I have always (with occasional, but brief, lapses) enjoyed being a pastor. But never this much. The experience of my maturity was now coupled with the energy of my youth, a combination I had not thought possible. The parts of pastoral work

I had done out of duty before, just because somebody had to do them, I now embraced with delight. I felt deep reservoirs within me, capacious and free flowing. I felt great margins of leisure around everything I did—conversations, meetings, letter writing, telephone calls. I felt I would never again be in a hurry. The sabbatical had done its work.

God cares for us by providing the sabbath. Indeed, he not only provides it but commands it. And, as Peterson suggests, it takes a command to "intervene in the vicious, accelerating, self-perpetuating cycle of faithless and graceless busyness, the only part of which we are conscious being our good intentions."

Think about and plan for your sabbath rest.

Worship

Spending time with God in corporate and private worship is another way of letting him take care of you. Both in worship and in solitude God communicates his love and presence.

In *Celebration of Discipline,* Richard Foster writes:

Loneliness is inner emptiness. Solitude is inner fulfillment. Solitude is not first a place but a state of mind and heart. Inward solitude will have outward manifestations. There will be the freedom to be alone, not in order to be away from people but in order to hear God better.

And concerning worship, Foster quotes William Temple, "To worship is to quicken the conscience by the holiness of God, to feed the mind with the truth of God, to purge the imagination by the beauty of God, *to open the heart to the love of God,* to devote the will to the purpose of God."

Making worship—worship with reverence and joy—a priority in life is a way to allow God to fill us, to nurture us, to revive and refresh us.

Let Yourself Hurt

Another practical way of letting God care for us is to give ourselves permission to grieve, to hurt, to feel loss and to not feel guilty about it. I use the phrase "give ourselves permission" intentionally. We begin by acknowledging to ourselves that it is okay to rest, that it is okay to grieve. God is ready to take care of us, but he does not force his care upon us. We choose to allow him to care for us by giving ourselves permission.

I belong to a small group of people who are important to me. In the course of just a couple years, members in that group have experienced agonizing losses. Jim and Carol watched her father die of cancer. Carolyn's oldest daughter, pregnant with her first child, was killed in a car accident. Pattie struggles with feeling worthless and with not even wanting to live. Mary watched a deep love relationship stall and become a friendship rather than move into marriage. Don and Patrice lost their first baby in the first trimester after having much difficulty getting pregnant at all.

They were all free to grieve. They each shared their pain openly. They allowed us to walk through it with them. There was no pretense. There was only truth.

Because they each gave themselves permission to grieve, all of us experienced deeply God's care and comfort. It did not alleviate the excruciating pain. In fact, looking at pain straight in the eye rather than averting it caused us to feel it even more intensely. But miracles occurred. As we share sorrow and pain, over time healing takes place. Our spirits are touched by God, and we grow.

Let Others Care for You
Finally, we let God take care of us by giving others permission to take care of us. We who are plagued with the I-have-to-take-care-of-myself or the I-have-to-take-care-of-others syndrome may have an especially hard time with this. Giving others permission to take care of us is a logical follow-up to allowing ourselves to grieve. To allow someone to care for us is to admit that we have needs.

Our Christian brothers and sisters are gifts from God. His love is lived out to us from others. When I receive care from a Christian friend, I receive care from God. Ecclesiastes says, "Two are better than one, because they have a good return for their work: If one falls down, his friend can help him up. But pity the man who falls and has no one to help him up! Also, if two lie together, they will keep warm. But how can one keep warm alone? Though one may be overpowered, two can defend themselves. A cord of three strands is not quickly broken" (4:9-12).

One simple way to allow others to help is to delegate responsibilities to others. It means letting go of the "If I don't do it, it won't get done—or at least it won't get done right" myth. When we not only allow others to share responsibilities, but also express appreciation for how they accomplished the task, so much the better.

Allowing someone to help you is good for the other person as well as for you. That person's self-esteem is enhanced. You create a sense of mutuality and an environment of openness and vulnerability. You also are training someone in how to care for another.

My friend, Carolyn, who lost her daughter in an automobile accident, describes her experience of letting others care for her:

For fifteen years going to Bible study was like going to work. I attended four small groups a week. I wrote the schedules, arranged for leaders, searched for baby-sitters, made suggestions to hostesses, supplied choices for curriculum, followed up newcomers, researched knotty theological issues, counseled people with personal problems, and planned group holiday celebrations. Because I write inductive Bible studies for a living, these four groups were my laboratory, the place where I worked. Sure everybody else pitched in and helped. But they helped *me*—I carried the primary burden. . . .

Then came the year that a car accident killed our oldest daughter, pregnant with our first grandchild. A short time later, our oldest son was hospitalized because of a mental breakdown. At first, I decided to drop out of all my small groups. After all, I couldn't predict my emotional condition, or whether I would have to make a quick trip to the hospital. I didn't feel like an authority on anything that required faith. . . .

But I changed my mind. I stayed with my neighborhood groups, the groups where I worked. Or rather they stayed with me. Leaders, hostesses, sitters emerged. For years I had taught that groups need to become self-sufficient, not dependent on any one person. Now I experienced it.

The people from these small groups who had cared for our family the week of Sheri's death—with food, housing, transportation, hugs and tears—now took over the Bible studies. And they ministered to me. Sometimes I just sat. Sometimes I cried. Sometimes I told the same stories about Sheri over and over. They listened and cared and prayed. And God's work went on.

It wasn't easy for me or them. Sometimes I thought if I had to listen to one more minute of normal cheery conversation I would bolt for the door. (I didn't. But I warned them that I might.) Sometimes they just held me—like the time I came straight to an evening group after an hour of tearfully making my way through the grocery store with Sheri's favorite foods leaping off the shelves at me with every turn of my cart.

I knew I was beginning to recover when a song sheet from one of the groups caught my eye from its discarded spot on the dining-room table. For the first time in weeks, I felt like singing praise—a little. The first time I led a group again, I prepared with all the nervousness of a novice. During the study I could feel others in the group helping guide the discussion as if I were a first time leader, and I appreciated their care. As the year wore on, we all gained insight into suffering, theirs and mine. And we grew in our trust of a God who, for reasons known only to himself, does not protect us from pain but instead enters into suffering with us."[1]

When we give others permission to care for us, God cares for us too.

---

[1]Jim and Carol Plueddeman, *Pilgrims in Progress: Growing Through Groups* (Wheaton, Ill.: Harold Shaw, 1990), pp. 137-39.

Questions for Groups or Individuals

1. In general, how willing would you say you are to let God care for you?

2. This chapter discusses specific ways that you can allow God to take care of you. How do you respond to them?

3. How would you describe your lifestyle? (harried? full of dread? full of contentment? steady?) Explain.

4. To what degree are you able to relax?

What affects this ability?

5. When do you feel most vibrant and able to move on with life enthusiastically?

6. What has been your experience with worship and/or solitude?

7. How readily do you share your pain with others?

8. When have you received God's care through another person taking care of you?

What was it like?

For Further Study:
Resources for Caring People, Caring for Emotional Needs.

10/Starting a Support Group

For individuals in local churches involved in ministry to people in crisis, small groups are essential for support. Christ's ministry on earth had as its cornerstone his meetings with the twelve disciples as a group. And the early New Testament church met together in small groups in homes where they shared their spiritual walk, material possessions, and passion for ministry to others.

A ministry of visitation to people in crisis may be demanding and confusing. As individuals struggle to find meaning in their pain, they may also challenge the helper's faith. People who care for others often feel "emptied out." Refueling comes when support and encouragement are offered by persons in a similar ministry.

Attempting a ministry to people in crisis by yourself can be devastating. I know of one man who took on such a ministry by himself in a local congregation. He did not last six months. He left totally overwhelmed by the needs he saw and the sense he could not help "these people" by himself.

Elements of Group Life

Commitment, vision and sharing are all important components of support groups. Additionally, the necessity for continued spiritual growth of individuals participating in ministry to persons in crisis is critical. Understanding the dynamics of a personal walk with the Lord and receiving personal support in that process enables the helper to better empathize with others, and to be a better support to people in crisis.

Studying particular portions of Scripture is a vital ingredient to supporting one another in ministry. Such studies keep the team focused, realistic in their plans and purposes and teach them the how-to's of drawing near to God and growing in their relationship with Christ. The Word of God will not return void (Is 55:10-11). That is a definite promise to us from God. A stimulating small group experience provides a context that can set this promise in motion.

During a crisis, people are often more open to communicating with God as they perceive him. However, not everyone you offer support to will understand the nature of prayer. Often even church members find that they have never really learned the discipline of prayer. Once a situation is out of their control, they become concerned about learning it. As a caregiver, you may also find that you have much to learn about prayer.

Prayer in the context of the small group is a way to help one another honestly approach God's grace. Praying together gives that sense of special unity of purpose and an increased sense of the power of God to intervene in any situation.

The psalmist often uses such phrases as "the Lord will hear my prayer and he will answer me," and "the Lord has heard my prayer, and he will deliver me." The psalmist was sure and confident. He knew God was listening.

Do we believe that God will hear and answer us? If we do, we must pray with assurance and confidence. Begin to look for answers, realizing that even in the answers "no," "wait" or "continue to intercede" there is blessing and evidence of the mighty working of God. Look for it, wait for it, rejoice in it. As a group, you will be learning the purpose and power of prayer, especially in your ministry to others.

A plan to have some fun together is also important to group life. Simple gatherings of the group for "fun and games" go a long way in helping you get to know one another, establish and enhance trust, and keep perspective.

Additionally, networking with Christian professionals is important for your group. If you have in your church or community Christian physicians, psychologists, counselors, nurses or teachers, get to know them. Build trust with your group and those professionals. Training sessions for your group's continuing growth could include seminars by professionals on various issues that confront you as you minister to people. See if some of the professionals may wish to be on a referral list that could be given to individuals or families in need.

Finally, read, read, read! There are wonderful books available by Christians who have suffered or gone through crises and who share their experiences. There are also many books that can heighten your understanding of your role as a helper, as well as prayer and Bible study. You may want to choose some books for the whole group to read and discuss as part of their growth and development as compassionate Christians. At the back of this book, you'll find a list to get you started.

Group Leadership

Essential to the success of a ministry to people in crisis and to any small groups is having a designated leader. The leader should be chosen carefully by the pastor or other lay leaders of the church who have wisdom and discernment about character, commitment, experience and skill. Ideal candidates should be committed to:

1. Jesus Christ as Lord and his mission and ministry.
2. The local church ministry.
3. Scripture as the primary resource for the Christian walk.
4. Personal and corporate spiritual gifts.
5. Small group experience.
6. The discipline of personal and group prayer.
7. Nurturing healthy human relationships.
8. Working through conflicts to forgiveness and healing.
9. The desire to develop and share group leadership roles.

Healthy small group experiences are dependent on healthy leadership. Leaders must be nurtured themselves while they learn to nurture others. Small groups used as part of ministry teams should have pastoral input, encouragement, training and open communication. Part of the leader's role will be to know when the pastor is needed and when the elders of the church need to be called in to anoint or to receive confession or at times to give support in death.

The following are some of the key steps the leader will follow in getting a support group together:

Pre-Group Preparation
☐ Experiencing a sense of concern and calling
☐ Sharing this concern and calling with your pastor
☐ Investigating the specific needs
☐ Praying for the actual vision and for others to share your concern
☐ Honestly assessing your own spiritual life
☐ Gaining knowledge of how others have started similar ministries
☐ Reading and personal preparation
☐ Sharing your vision with others, asking them to pray about their own involvement
☐ Selecting a team

Suggested Format for Meetings
☐ Prayer
☐ Bible study
☐ Sharing of personal areas of growth, as well as needs and concerns for prayer
☐ Sharing the needs of those you are helping for prayer (as appropriate)

The leader may want to report back to pastoral staff as needed and organize some continuing education programs.

Branching Out
As your ministry group matures and grows you may find that group members need to become facilitators for other needed groups. As you minister to persons in crisis, you may find the need to establish particular types of support groups. These groups may focus on the special needs of those who are bereaved, divorced, and those who are coming out of drug or alcohol addiction, homosexuality or other sexual addictions.

In these kinds of groups, individuals with the same personal issues come together to attempt to understand one another and to support one another through sharing experiences and praying together. Feelings of aloneness are relieved as people see that they are not the only ones who feel a certain way or have needs which are brought on by particular situations in their lives.

Members of the original group may need to serve as leaders until someone from within the group emerges as a mature leader. These special needs groups may be short-term, reactivating only when there appears to be a need, or they may continue and become a major off-shoot of your continuing ministry.

Resource One: Record Keeping

A systematic ministry of visitation requires some form of record-keeping. The records kept provide consistency, and help to personalize your interaction during the time of the visit. A card file system is probably the easiest and cheapest forms to use for such records. The cards should be kept in a safe place to provide confidentiality.

Cards kept for people who have long-term illnesses or for the elderly homebound or nursing homebound should include such information as birthdays and anniversaries. These special days can be shared with the whole group or congregation so that cards and notes can be sent and the person can feel like part of the whole church.

An additional piece of information you might include on these cards is the length of the person's membership in that particular church. Knowing the "saints" who kept your congregation on track or provided for the building and its facilities and services will be an encouragement to your own faith.

People who will be visited weekly or monthly can be catalogued by day of the week or day of the month. That way anyone responsible for visiting that day has quick access to who should be visited and any special information needed about that individual.

Some visiting teams bring small cakes or cookies or candies or a flower when they visit. This is not a necessary aspect of this ministry. Your time is gift enough. If your team chooses to provide these special treats, they will also be much appreciated. However, be careful of special diets people may be on for particular health problems.

You might keep a record of likes and dislikes for certain foods, favorite flowers or special portions of Scripture on the card.

These cards can also be used as prayer reminders as your group meets to share, study and pray. Be faithful in lifting the specific needs of each of the persons being visited to the Lord in prayer. And, remember to pray for yourselves for spiritual wisdom, discernment and sensitivity to others.

God bless you as you take in earnest the ministry of reconciliation and healing that the Lord has called us to perform.

The following are some samples of how to do visitation cards:

Long-Term Card. For those who are elderly or chronically ill.

Name: Hospital:

Address: Returned home:

Phone: Birthday:

                                                           Anniversary:

Comments regarding general condition:
  (deaf, blind, confined to bed, etc.)

Dates visited: Day to be visited:

  (month/day/year)   Visitor's name:

List the individual's *likes* and *dislikes* on the reverse side.

Short-term. For those who are acutely ill.

Name: Hospital:

Address: Returned home:

                                                           Phone:

Comments regarding illness:

Dates visited: Visitor's name:

Resource Two: When Professional Help Is Needed

An important part of helping people is knowing when and how to get professional counseling help. The following symptoms may indicate that someone is dealing with problems too difficult to handle alone:

☐ The problem persists for many months, with no resolution in sight.

☐ The person feels as if he or she "has all the answers" but doesn't know how to apply them to his or her situation.

☐ The person feels very depressed for several weeks at a time for no apparent reason.

☐ Thoughts of suicide or other abnormal behavior occur frequently.

If professional counseling is necessary, the following are suggestions you can give someone to help in finding a counselor:

☐ The relationship between the counselor and client is very unique and very intimate. Look for someone you feel comfortable with. If the first counselor doesn't work out, look for another.

☐ Ask a friend, a pastor, a doctor or someone else you respect for a recommendation for a good counselor. Board certification is one thing to look for, but personal recommendation is probably even more important. If you have no one to ask, looking in the yellow pages of the phone book is better than not going at all.

☐ Try to speak with the counselor by phone before the first appointment. Even a phone conversation will give you an idea of whether or not you will be able to relate to the counselor. Ask about his or her professional certification, and ask what approach the counselor uses. Ask about the person's professional background (this should tell you how much experience the person has had in counseling). Ask too how the counselor's spiritual values influence his or her counseling.

☐ It is good if your counselor is a believer, but don't assume that a non-Christian counselor cannot be helpful. Likewise, don't assume that just because someone is a Christian that he or she will be a good counselor.

☐ Once you begin to see the counselor, ask for an assessment of your situation and the counselor's tentative goals for your counseling experience. The counselor won't be able to hand you "all the answers" but should be insightful and goal oriented.

☐ When you go for counseling, be as open, as honest and as specific as you can be about your own needs and feelings. Your participation in your counseling experience is even more important than your counselor's in terms of the success of your therapy.*

---

*Adapted from *Disciplemakers' Handbook* by Alice Fryling (Downers Grove, Ill.: InterVarsity Press, 1989), pp. 125-26.

Further Reading

Crisis and Death

Bayly, Joseph. *The Last Thing We Talk about*. Elgin, Ill.: David C. Cook, 1969.

Bayly, Joseph. *Psalms of My Life*. Wheaton, Ill.: Tyndale, 1969.

Boom, Corrie ten. *He Cares, He Comforts*. Old Tappan, N.J.: Revell, 1977.

_____. *The Hiding Place*. Minneapolis, Minn.: Chosen Books, 1971. London: Hodder and Stoughton, 1976.

Clarkson, Margaret. *Grace Grows Best in Winter*. Grand Rapids, Mich.: Eerdmans, 1972.

Claypool, John. *Tracks of a Fellow Struggler*. Waco, Tex.: Word, 1974.

Eareckson, Joni. *Joni*. Grand Rapids, Mich.: Zondervan, 1976. London: STL, 1983.

_____. *A Step Further*. Grand Rapids, Mich.: Zondervan, 1978. London: Pickering and Inglis, 1984.

Hong, Edna. *Turn Over Any Stone*. San Francisco, Calif.: Harper & Row, 1990.

Kübler-Ross, Elisabeth. *On Death and Dying*. New York, N.Y.: MacMillan Co., 1969. London: Tavistock Publications, 1970

Landorf, Joyce. *Mourning Song*. Old Tappan, N.J.: Revell, 1974.

Lewis, C. S. *A Grief Observed*. Greenwich, Conn.: Seabury Press, 1965. London: Faber, 1966.

_____. *The Problem of Pain*. New York, N.Y.: Macmillan Co., 1962. London: Fontana, 1957.

Marshall, Catherine. *Beyond Ourselves*. New York, N.Y.: McGraw- Hill Co. Inc., 1961. London: Hodder and Stoughton, 1969.

Schaeffer, Edith. *Affliction*. Old Tappan, N.J.: Revell, 1978.

Swihart, Phillip. *The Edge of Death*. Downers Grove, Ill.: InterVarsity Press, 1978.

Tournier, Paul. *Learning to Grow Old*. New York, N.Y.: Harper and Row, 1972. London: SCM Press, 1972.

Westberg, Granger E. *Good Grief*. Philadelphia, Penn.: Fortress Press, 1962.

White, John. *Parents in Pain*. Downers Grove, Ill.: InterVarsity Press, 1979. Leicester: Inter-Varsity Press, 1980.

Worden, Mary Jane. *Early Widow*. Downers Grove, Ill.: InterVarsity Press, 1989.

Yancey, Philip. *Disappointment with God*. Grand Rapids, Mich.: Zondervan, 1988.

_____ . *Where Is God When It Hurts?* Grand Rapids, Mich.: Zondervan, 1979.

Involvement and Intervention

Anderson, S. J. *When Someone Wants to Die*. Downers Grove, Ill: IVP, 1988.

Berry, Carmen R. *When Helping You Is Hurting Me*. San Francisco, Calif.: Harper & Row, 1988.

Collins, Gary. *How To Be a People Helper*. Santa Ana, Calif.: Vision House, 1976.

Fenton, Horace. *When Christians Clash*. Downers Grove, Ill.: InterVarsity Press, 1987. Published in the UK as *The Peacemakers*. Leicester: Inter-Varsity Press, 1988.

Swindoll, Charles. *For Those Who Hurt*. Portland, Ore.: Multnomah, 1977.

Welter, Paul. *How to Help a Friend*. Wheaton, Ill.: Tyndale, Inc., 1978.

Westberg, Granger. *Nurse, Pastor, and Patient*. Rock Island, Ill.: Augustana Press, 1955.

Wright, Norman H. *Crisis Counseling*. San Bernadino, Calif.: Here's Life, 1985.

Worthington, Everett. *When Someone Asks for Help*. Downers Grove, Ill.: InterVarsity Press, 1982.

Recovery Issues

Beattie, Melody. *Codependent No More*. San Francisco, Calif.: Harper & Row, 1988.

Conway, Jim. *Adult Children of Legal and Emotional Divorce*. Downers Grove, Ill.: Inter-Varsity Press, 1990.

May, Gerald. *Addiction and Grace*. San Francisco, Calif.: Harper & Row, 1988. London: Harper and Row, 1990.

Ogilvie, Lloyd. *12 Steps to Living Without Fear*. Waco, Tex.: Word, 1987.

Ryan, Dale and Juanita. *Recovery from Codependency, Recovery from Loss, Recovery from Distorted Images of God*. Life Recovery Guides. Downers Grove, Ill.: InterVarsity Press, 1990. London: Scripture Union.

Seamands, David. *Healing Grace*. Wheaton, Ill.: Victor Books, 1988.

_____ . *Healing of Memories*. Wheaton, Ill.: Victor Books, 1985.

Wilson, Sandra. *Released from Shame*. Downers Grove, Ill.: InterVarsity Press, 1990.

Self-Understanding and Growth

Augsburger, David. *Caring Enough to Confront*. Glendale, Calif.: Gospel Light Publications, 1973.

————. *Freedom of Forgiveness.* Chicago, Ill.: Moody Press, 1970. Amersham: Scripture Press, 1989.

————. *When Enough Is Enough.* Ventura, Calif.: Regal, 1984.

Beers, V. G. *Turn Your Hurts into Healing.* New Jersey: Fleming H. Revell, 1988.

Buckingham, J. *A Way through the Wilderness.* New Jersey: Chosen Books, 1986. Eastbourne: Kingsway, 1984.

Ginott, Haim G. *Between Parent and Child.* New York, N.Y.: MacMillan, 1965.

MacDonald, Gordon. *Rebuilding Your Broken World.* Nashville: Thomas Nelson, 1988. Crowborough: Highland, 1988.

Miller, Keith. *The Becomers.* Waco, Tex.: Word, 1973.

Osborne, Cecil. *You're in Charge.* Waco, Tex.: Word, 1973.

Powell, John. *The Secret of Staying in Love.* Allen, Tex.: Tabor Publications, rev. ed. 1990. Harlow: Argus, 1976.

————. *Why Am I Afraid to Love?* Allen, Tex.: Tabor Publications, rev. ed. 1990. London: Fontana, 1975.

————. *Why Am I Afraid to Tell You Who I Am?* Allen, Tex.: Tabor Publications, rev. ed. 1990. London: Fontana: 1975.

Swihart, Judson. *How Do You Say, "I Love You"?* Downers Grove, Ill.: InterVarsity Press, 1977.

Trobisch, Walter. *Love Yourself.* Downers Grove, Ill.: InterVarsity Press, 1976.

Spiritual Development

Adeney, Carol (ed.) *This Morning with God.* Downers Grove, Ill.: InterVarsity Press, 1972.

Conyers, A. J. *How to Read the Bible.* Downers Grove, Ill.: InterVarsity Press, 1986.

Fish, Sharon, and Shelly, Judith Allen. *Spiritual Care: The Nurse's Role.* Downers Grove, Ill.: InterVarsity Press, 1978.

Packer, J. I. *Knowing God.* Downers Grove, Ill.: InterVarsity Press, 1973. London: Hodder and Stoughton, rev. ed., 1975.

Shelly, Judith Allen. *Caring in Crisis.* Downers Grove, Ill: InterVarsity Press, 1979.

Stibbs, Alan M., ed. *Search the Scriptures.* Downers Grove, Ill.: InterVarsity Press, 1949, rev. 1967. Leicester: Inter-Varsity Press, 5th ed., 1967.

Wald, Oletta. *The Joy of Discovery.* Minneapolis, Minn.: Bible Banner Press, 1956.

White, John. *Daring to Draw Near.* Downers Grove, Ill.: InterVarsity Press, 1977. Published in the UK as *People in Prayer.* Leicester: Inter-Varsity Press, 1978.

Willoughby, Ro. *The Quiet Time Companion.* Downers Grove, Ill.: InterVarsity Press, 1988. Published in the UK as *Adventure with God.* Leicester: Inter-Varsity Press, 1990.

Caring People Bible Studies from InterVarsity Press
By Phyllis J. Le Peau

Handbook for Caring People (coauthored by Bonnie J. Miller). This book provides simple, time-tested principles for dealing with the pain, the questions and the crises people face. You will get the basic tools for communication plus some practical suggestions. Questions for group discussion are at the end of each chapter.

Resources for Caring People. Through God, we have the resources we need to help others. God has given us Scripture, prayer, the Holy Spirit, listening and acceptance. This guide will show you how he works through people like you every day. 8 studies.

The Character of Caring People. The key to caring is character. These Bible studies will show you how to focus on the gifts of caring which God has given you—such as hospitality, generosity and encouragement. 8 studies.

Caring for Spiritual Needs. A relationship with God. Meaning and purpose. Belonging. Love. Assurance. These are just some of the spiritual needs that we all have. This Bible study guide will help you learn how these needs can be met in your life and in the lives of others. 9 studies.

Caring for Emotional Needs. We think we have to act like we have it all together, yet sometimes we are lonely, afraid or depressed. Christians have emotional needs just like everyone else. This Bible study guide shows how to find emotional health for ourselves and how to help others. 9 studies.

Caring for Physical Needs. When we are sick or when our basic needs for food, clothing and adequate housing are not being met, our whole being—body, spirit and emotion—is affected. When we care for the physical needs of others, we are showing God's love. These Bible studies will help you learn to do that. 8 studies.

Caring for People in Conflict. Divided churches. Broken friendships. Angry children. Torn marriages. We all have to deal with conflict and the emotions which accompany it. These studies will show you how God can bring healing and reconciliation. 9 studies.

Caring for People in Grief. Because sin brought death into the world, we all have to look into death's ugly face at one time or another. These Bible studies cover the issues which consume those who are grieving—fear, peace, grace and hope—and show you how to provide them with comfort. 9 studies.